TH

To Fraser,
a Shankley
man and
Liverpool fan.

All the best,

Chris

Thanks Shanks

How Bill Shankly
bought me an Education
... and Denis Law
kicked me in the shins

David Kershaw

as told to Chris Arnot

This edition published 2017 by:
Takahe Publishing Ltd.
Registered Office:
77 Earlsdon Street, Coventry CV5 6EL

Copyright ©Chris Arnot 2017

ISBN 978-1-908837-09-7

TAKAHE PUBLISHING LTD.

2017

To the memory of an inspirational manager whose perception went beyond football, whose generosity changed my life and helped me to change the lives of others.

CONTENTS

Chapter	Title	Page
1	Childhood Happiness "oop 't' top"	1
2	Eleven minus	17
3	Damned with faint praise	29
4	Steak'n'chips'n' Roker Park	41
5	Great Scots at Cleckheaton	51
6	Saturday night and Sunday yawning	61
7	Bill picks up the bill	73
8	An Eccles cake at Anfield	83
9	Cricket, unlovely cricket	95
10	Goodbye Mum, hello Brum	107
11	Love's Young Dream in Summer Lane	119
12	The Joys of Hereford and Handsworth	129
13	Wedded Bliss with a Cat that Hissed	143
14	Taming the Tigers and Gaining Respect	153
15	Finding a Nest before Flying Away	163
16	Sending Ourselves to Coventry	175
17	Gaining Promotion and Heading for the Top	189
...	Postscript	203
...	Pictures from the Past	209

FOREWORD

"To say that these men paid their shillings to watch 22 hirelings kick a ball is merely to say that ... Hamlet is so much paper and ink," wrote that redoubtable Yorkshireman JB Priestley at the beginning of an evocative passage in the Good Companions in 1929.

The team that "these men" followed was Bruddersfield Town FC, and it will come as no surprise that he came upon the name by conflating two fiercely independent outposts of west Yorkshire. One was Huddersfield and the other Bradford, the city where David Kershaw was born just after Priestley had finished his wartime broadcasts for the BBC. By the mid-1950s, he was playing for Huddersfield Town's youth team when a "skinny, squinty kid" arrived from Aberdeen. His name was Denis Law and he would go on to become one of football's immortals. So would another Scot who took over the management of the club soon after Law's arrival.

I knew nothing about the involvement of Bill Shankly in the life of David, or rather Councillor Kershaw, until I popped round to see him about a threat by the local authority to withdraw funding from our beloved public library in Earlsdon, Coventry. It was only when I was about to leave that it came out in conversation that libraries meant a lot to him as one who had left school aged 14, semi-literate with no qualifications whatsoever.

To say that I was staggered by this revelation would be putting it mildly.

How, then, had he become such a celebrated head teacher in the 1980s and '90s? How had he transformed Coundon Court School from chaos into an Ofsted topper of the local league tables? Why had the marked improvement in so many Coventry primary schools coincided with his chairmanship of the City Council's Education Committee? And why, in his mid-70s, was he still being asked by the Department of Education to sort out problem schools in other parts of the country?

By now my journalistic antennae were twitching. One of the things that I love about Coventry is that it's full of people from somewhere else with good stories to tell. Apart from anything else, this was a tale involving two footballing legends from my youth, when I'd still cared passionately about our national winter game. I may be seven years younger than the venerable Kershaw, but I can still remember paying a shilling ("boys' price") for the privilege of nearly being crushed to death on the Holte End at Villa Park when the visitors were the Spurs double-winning side. Plus Jimmy Greaves.

The more David and I talked, the more it became apparent that this was a story that shouldn't be confined to a restricted space in a newspaper or magazine. After all, it's not often that professional football is coupled with a heart-warming story about the transformative effects of education. There was a book in it.

But who was going to publish it?

Not AA Travel, that was for sure, even if they had commissioned my railway adventure, Small Island by

Foreword

Little Train, and published it earlier this year. Nor Aurum, publisher of my books on lost cricket grounds, breweries and mines. And not Stepbeach, who had brought out Fields of Dreams – even though my last visit to Huddersfield had involved searching for the disc marking the centre-circle of the Town's former ground in a shopping-centre car park off Leeds Road.

Step forward at this point Steve Hodder who runs Takahe Publishing as well as tackling cryptic crosswords and studiously analysing the racing pages in my local pub, the Royal Oak. Yes, he'd do it. No, I wasn't going to make much money from it but what the hell. For once I wouldn't be travelling all over the country in the cause of research. I'd be walking about three-quarters of a mile whenever I needed to listen to another fascinating episode of an absorbing saga. David's life struck a chord with me as someone who remembered soporific Sundays in the 1950s, playing cricket and football in the street, as well as the divisions that the eleven-plus threw up between children who were otherwise close neighbours.

So many thanks to him for sharing his memories in full for the first time. Not easy for a "cussed Yorkshireman" who has been reluctant to admit that he'd needed help to get on the educational ladder. Thanks also to Steve for his assiduous copy-reading; to cartoonists John Russell with helpful input from my old mate Pete Dredge; to Vivien Kershaw for reminding her husband of key dates in their family history; and to my own wife Jackie who has kept me well supplied with her delicious home-made soup while I've been in my office in the loft.

Thanks Shanks

Having the chance to write this book has been an unexpected pleasure. The chances of finding it in our local library, mind you, are about as likely as Huddersfield Town merging with Bradford City or even David's beloved Bradford Park Avenue FC. Council funding has been largely withdrawn. It's now open only three and a half days a week and wouldn't be open at all but for the stalwart efforts of volunteers.

As Bill Shankly would never have said, you can't win 'em all.

Chris Arnot,
November 2017.

CHAPTER ONE

Childhood Happiness "oop 't' top"

Sundays were not fun days in our house. Not in many other houses either, I suspect, in those grim and pinched post-war days when "I were a lad" in Bradford. "'T' mill oop 't' road" was eerily quiet. The shops were shut. Churches were open, of course, and so were Sunday schools. I was despatched to the one closest to our house as soon as I was old enough. It happened to be a Methodist Sunday school and what I absorbed there stayed with me for the rest of my life. Would that I could say the same for my primary school. Or my secondary school for that matter. I left both barely literate – a state of affairs that was overcome only by the intervention of a legendary football manager who inspired many a life and transformed mine.

The story of how that came about will be at the core of this book. But for now let's take a peep back through the lace curtains of my childhood home. Or more aptly, perhaps, let's listen at the keyhole. Two sounds would greet my return from Sunday school. One was my Dad snoring, the other was some brass band or crooner emanating from the Light Programme to which our substantial, walnut-veneer "wireless" was tuned while my mother did the ironing.

I'd settle down on the settee and flick through my football magazine, looking at the pictures because I couldn't read the words beneath. Oh, what a brief but welcome treat it was when the music prescribed by Lord Reith's BBC was interrupted by a repeat of the most recent episode of Dick Barton, Special Agent, first broadcast on the previous Thursday evening just as I was being sent to bed.

Sunday afternoon was when we intruded into the hallowed sanctuary of the front "parlour" as a family, although my younger sister Ann tended to disappear into her bedroom at the earliest opportunity. The only other time Mum ventured in here was to polish the wireless, the bureau and sideboard within an inch of their lives or to play cards with her friends when they came round on Thursday or Saturday evenings. The parlour would be full of gossip and giggles on those occasions, particularly on Thursdays when it was "ladies only". No brass band music. And no snoring. Dad would make himself scarce instead of reclining in a substantial armchair, mouth open and head resting on an antimacassar.

Childhood Happiness "oop t top"

Snores emanating from the male of the species were hardly unusual on those soporific Sunday afternoons. They tended to be the consequences of English roast beef preceded by English draught ale. Pubs were allowed to open, but only between the hours of seven and ten in the evening and twelve and two at lunchtime – or rather "dinnertime" as it was referred to in our neck of the woods. Snugs and smoke rooms, bars and "vaults" would be almost entirely populated by men. As for the "Gents Only", well the clue was in the name.

Some 'gents' would weave their way home only after closing time, then complain that the beef was overdone before retiring to the parlour to slump and rumble volubly for the rest of the afternoon. At least my Dad wasn't one to complain. He was a gentle man as well as a gentleman, warm-hearted yet quiet and self-contained (while he was awake at least).

Mind you, he'd still have had most of the meat that was going on Sunday dinnertime. Brisket was the cheapest of the beef cuts and Mum had a regular weekly order with the butcher. She would then make the joint last for at least four days. On Mondays, Tuesdays and Wednesdays we'd have it cold with mashed potato, soggy cabbage, lumpy swede and some Yorkshire chutney. On

Sundays, however, the real meal deal for us kids was the Yorkshire pudding.

Our tiny kitchen was dominated by a big old-fashioned range and Mum prided herself on the way she could get the Yorkshires to rise in there. They spread, too, right across the plate. Filled with onion gravy they were a meal in themselves. Just as well. Having the Yorkshire pud as a "starter" was a longstanding tradition. The idea was to fill up the kids and hence prevent them from asking for too much meat.

A small electric oven had somehow been wedged into the kitchen alongside the range. It was used for one dish and one dish only. We had rice pudding every day of the year, with a deviation into stewed apple and custard once in a blue moon. Every night before she went to bed, Mum would steep the rice by covering it with water and putting it in the range, which remained warm into the early hours. As soon as she got up in the morning, she'd cover it with milk before sprinkling nutmeg on the top and leaving it ready to shove into the electric cooker every dinnertime. You'd think I'd never want to look another rice pud in the face, but I still love it to this day – if it's done properly, that is, with a bit of a skin on it.

What you might call Mum's *pièce de résistance* (if you

came from Bordeaux rather than Bradford) was her fish and chips. Every Friday dinnertime we'd rush home from school to be greeted by the gorgeous aroma of potatoes and batter plunged into boiling beef dripping. Concerns about the effect on the heart were a long way in the future. It was dripping or "nowt" in chip shops all over Yorkshire, and it was in one of those shops that Mum had learnt how to cook with it. She lived above the 'chippie' from the age of 13, having been kicked out of the family home at Birtley, near Newcastle, because it was becoming too overcrowded. Her father was a miner in the Durham coalfield and her mother was almost permanently pregnant. When the ninth child was born, it was deemed that "young Alice", the oldest child, would have to move out to make room and live with relatives in White Abbey, near Bradford city centre.

She had to earn her keep, needless to say, and Alice was soon learning how to fold a piece of fish into batter and how to wrap it up, with a "penn'orth" of chips or two, in the previous evening's front and back page of the Telegraph and Argus. She was soon passing on her recently acquired know-how to an even younger teenage lad who learnt his trade at this shop. He'd go on to make a bit of a name for himself. Made a bit of money, too, did Harry Ramsden.

Thanks Shanks

Mum didn't tell me about this until many years later, so I never had the chance to meet the redoubtable Mr Ramsden. The nearest I came to it was tucking into a fish supper under the chandeliers at his oak-panelled prime premises in Guiseley.

As for the chippie where Mum taught him the tricks of the trade, it's now a very different shop selling beautiful saris. But it was there that she bonded with Jarratt Kershaw over a piece of battered haddock. A good Yorkshire name, Jarratt. Pity my Dad hated it. He much preferred to be called Jack. Quite appropriately, as it turned out. After passing his 11-plus, going to grammar school and landing a steady job with the City Council as a rent collector, he became a Jack Tar with the Royal Navy. World War Two had broken out and Mum didn't see much of him for the best part of six years.

He came home on leave twice, and I was born nine months after the first time. Ann didn't come along until after he returned from the war. Like many a serviceman who had witnessed terrible events, he never spoke about it. Until two days before he died, that is, when he was 90 years old. He told me that the most emotional moment of his life was when his friend threw himself overboard just off the coast of Japan. Suffered from shell-shock, apparently. As for my father, he was hard of hearing for the rest of his life and almost deaf by the time he died. The cause wasn't difficult to imagine. He had been close to the sound of gunfire and explosions in a confined space for a long time.

Having been born in 1942, you might imagine that I can remember bombs falling on Bradford. But thankfully I can't. Nor do I recall street parties on VE Day. One of my earliest memories is of the Anderson shelter being taken down in the back garden and some of the corrugated iron being used for the roof of a new shed.

The City Council did that, I gathered. Why I know not. What I do know is that we lived on the Cooperville Estate on Horton Bank Top, a thousand feet above sea level. We were right on the edge of town, four miles from the centre of Bradford. The bus took 40 minutes to cover those four miles because the hills were so steep that it had to go most of the way in first gear.

Cooperville was built between the wars under a government scheme. The City Council collected the rent, which had risen to the dizzy heights of five quid by the 1990s when my father was still living there. Nearly 50 years earlier it would have been a fraction of that.

For a comparative pittance you were granted facilities

that many of the pre-war working class could only have dreamed about. A small garden, front and back, for a start. Even better: a small bathroom with an inside toilet. There was a box-room upstairs, too, just about big enough to house a single bed. I slept there while Ann had a slightly larger room beyond Mum and Dad's. Three bedrooms then . . . well, two and a bit.

Downstairs, as I've already mentioned, was that tiny kitchen with the large range that provided warmth as well as brisket, Yorkshire pud and fish and chips. Central heating was a distant dream. The kitchen was Mum's domain, needless to say. She shoved the food through a hatch into a dining area that an estate agent would describe as "compact".

The mill was nearby and the deafening din emanating from it was the background music to our lives. The vast majority of people on the estate worked there, the men booted, mufflered and capped for most of the year and the women in pinnies and headscarves. They started work at 7.30 in the morning but had to rush home at mid-day to get the "dinner" on. Then they'd go back until 4.30 in the afternoon, bent over great lengths of wool to mend any faults in it. The process was known as "burling" and it was a skilled darning operation. Yet it was almost like slave labour as they were paid piece-work rates according to how many lengths they mended.

The men's jobs were to work heavy machinery and hump about those heavy bundles of wool. They were the first out of the door come 4.30. Their wives came out en masse once they'd left and headed home to get the "tea" on as quickly as possible. In many cases, they knew that their men-folk would want to shovel something down before setting off for any one of the three pubs on the estate and be there for opening time.

Not surprisingly, Dad was seen as a bit different in this context. Not only was he a former grammar-school boy; he also went to work in a collar and tie. He was a very capable man, who could do the crossword in News Chronicle in a matter of minutes, but he had no ambition whatsoever. A steady job and a pension was all he wanted and, in those days, a job in local government was a job for life. Thankfully he didn't have to collect rents on our estate.

Unlike my mother, who was noisy and boisterous, he wanted a quiet life with set routines. He'd come home at the end of the week and hand over the housekeeping money to Mum, who had a little box with different sections in for food, clothing, heating and holidays. But he obviously kept back a bit for himself. Every Friday evening, without fail, he and a couple of mates would set off for a pint or two in the Dolphin. It was a two-mile walk away but slightly more upmarket than the 'boozers' on the estate. Even had a lounge bar, if you please.

And every Saturday afternoon, without fail, he'd set off for Bradford Park Avenue with me alongside him. Always the same spot; always the same mates of Dad around us. Football in the winter months, cricket in the summer. If the first team were away, we'd watch the seconds. There was an imposing stand in the middle with the football ground was on one side and the cricket ground on the other. Not the most idyllic of cricket settings, it must be said, but the aesthetics of the game were hardly a priority in the Bradford League. Brian Close and Ray Illingworth learnt their trade in that uncompromising, win-at-all-costs environment, and they were my cricketing heroes. Closey signed for Yorkshire in 1949, when I was seven, and Illy two years later. Like Fred Trueman and Bob Appleyard, they seemed to relish the county's regular visits to Bradford where the crowd was substantial, knowledgeable and voluble.

The cricket ground is still there, just about, and there are plans to redevelop it. As for the football pitch that so fired my imagination and attracted crowds of over 20,000, that's now under a supermarket. In my day, Bradford Park Avenue was in the Third Division North, along with Bradford City. But unlike City, they dropped out of the League altogether in 1970 and went bankrupt four years later. The club has since made a comeback in one of the minor leagues. Different ground, mind you, for obvious reasons.

The 'ground' where I played football at every available opportunity was a patch of shale-covered wasteland enclosed by the garages that housed the few motor vehicles on the estate – the delivery vans used by local shopkeepers for trips to the market. Did they mind us booting one of those old heavy leather case balls up against the woodwork at regular intervals? Not really. But one or two of them took exception to us chalking cricket wickets on there, as we did every summer from May to early September. If they insisted on us rubbing off the chalk marks, we'd simply wait until they'd gone back to the shop before recreating the wickets on another door.

We played with a tennis ball at first but quickly graduated to one of those hard rubber balls that hurt like hell if it caught you on or just under the kneecap. Pads?

This wasn't the nets at Lord's, you know, and we weren't soft southerners. We quickly learnt to play like proper Yorkshiremen with a sound defensive technique.

Later I would become an opening batsman and wicketkeeper – a role that wasn't required in the days of playing up against a garage door, for obvious reasons. I could catch and I could trap a football. Kick one, too, further than anybody else. Never mind reading and writing; here was something that I could do. Being taller and burlier than anyone else, I quickly took on the role of solid defender with a rugged tackle. And if anyone got bruised in the process, I could smile away any threats of retaliation.

My size and ability at ball games earned me the respect of other boys, even though I never swore and was embarrassed in the company of girls. That Methodist Sunday school had taught me to keep a clean tongue and my mother had implanted a suspicion of the opposite sex. She was always warning me about their manipulative ways. After all, I was my mother's boy, the apple of her eye. And in her eyes I could do no wrong. Poor Ann was almost an afterthought. Mum used to shout and scream at her, much to my Dad's embarrassment. No wonder my sister left home at the earliest opportunity. She finished up running a very successful hairdressing business in Geneva, marrying a wealthy Swiss guy and living life to the full until she very sadly died of cancer in her 60s.

Ann obviously had plenty about her in terms of drive and initiative. Yet I was the one who was given all the maternal attention. And Mum used to talk about me constantly to her friends. One of those family friends was a big, bluff character known to us kids as "Uncle Eric". He was the foreman at Padgett's, the company paid by the government to build the estate in the first place and to do all the maintenance work required to keep it up to scratch. There were things I liked about Uncle Eric and things that I didn't. He could be great fun, teasing my mother unmercifully. Whenever he came round, he'd ask in a simpering voice "And how's my little David today?"

That didn't bother me. There were two things about Uncle Eric that did, however. One was the way I heard him talk to his wife. They lived just round the corner and she was a very gentle and quiet lady. We were leaving their house once and I remember him saying to her: "You have my dinner on the table when I get back. Otherwise there'll be trouble." I never felt comfortable with him again because he said it with such menace.

Then there was the racism that he espoused with such venom. "I took one of my mates to Bradford Royal Infirmary," I remember him telling a crowded room on one occasion. "It was full of them effing Pakis, all breeding like rabbits. They ought to effing well sort 'em out. This is our city." There were plenty of people nodding as he said it but inside I just knew that it was wrong.

A few years later, when I was about 12 or 14, two Pakistani families moved on to the estate. They lasted 24 hours. Their windows were smashed and they were threatened with even worse consequences. Bradford has a large Pakistani population but, as far as I can tell on those rare occasions when I drive back, there are none on that estate to this day.

Back in the early post-war period, when former "colonials" were being invited to come and work in the "mother country", my father used to collect rents in and around the city centre. Former mill workers had moved a little way out of a town and there were lots of empty properties that soon became ridiculously overcrowded. Dad came home and told me once: "I went to this house off Lumb Lane and there were men asleep in sleeping bags all across the floor. When I went back later, they'd gone to their shift and there'd be another lot in the sleeping bags. They're being exploited by the mill owners. It's not right, David. I'm going to report it."

Instinctively I knew it wasn't right either. But I didn't dwell on it at the time. All I sensed was that I was a lucky lad. I was living in comparative luxury with two parents who loved me, and able to indulge my love of sport at every opportunity. The only downside of my life (apart from Sunday afternoons in the parlour) was school. Like quite a few others, I was whacked with a pump for talking too much and not writing properly. Nobody picked up the fact that I hadn't been taught properly. And that included my wonderfully loving and caring parents. They just wanted me to be happy and they never went near the school from beginning to end. No wonder I never saw school as important. It was just a place to meet my friends and show off my sporting skills in the playground.

In other respects, my life couldn't have been much better. Until, that is, something happened that would have profound effects on my sense of self-worth as well as my prospects for many years to come.

Thanks Shanks

CHAPTER TWO

Eleven minus

I was still ten when the eleven plus exam rudely intruded into my childhood. Eleven minus a few months, in other words. To say that I was minus the necessary skills would have been putting it mildly. If I concentrated very hard, I could just about scratch out my name with one of those italic nibs-on-a-stick that you dunked into an inkwell embedded into the top right-hand corner of what might be termed an all-in-one desk. There was a fold-down wooden bench below a lift-up wooden lid with just about enough room for a normal-sized child to squeeze in between the restrictive metalwork holding it all together.

As I may have mentioned, I was not a normal-sized child. I was already a big, burly lad and it was hard enough to clamber in without banging my knee or scraping a shin. Once ensconced, I felt wedged – or rather trapped like a prisoner in the stocks, waiting for whatever was going to be thrown at me.

We'd been marched into the school hall, military-style, under strict surveillance. Our headmistress was a formidable figure who made the average sergeant-major barking orders at National Service recruits seem like a bit of a softy. Her hair was scraped back into a bun the size of an inverted megaphone and she had a voice that could make the roar of nearby mill machinery seem like a distant murmur.

As we'd crept in, two by two, she'd insisted on us being separated into single file. Then we'd had to parade around the edge of that vast and draughty hall, with its overwhelming smell of polish and carbolic and its high windows that admitted little light. We were expected to keep one shoulder brushing against the wall to ensure that we kept in line. Only once we'd done a complete circuit were we allowed – "QUIETLY!" – to approach the incarceration of those stocks-like desks.

The first things to be thrown at me once the head had finally allowed us to turn over our exam papers – "WAIT! WAIT!" – was an incomprehensible set of puzzles. More accurately, they were box-like patterns with parts missing. They had to be completed. None of which meant much to me. I took a few wild guesses and then, after about 10 minutes, put down my pen and looked straight ahead. The following 50 minutes seemed like an eternity. As far as I could tell, through occasional surreptitious glances to left and right, everybody else seemed to have their heads down, scratching away with those nibs. One or two exceptions became apparent after a while but we daren't look at one another, let alone fidget. Clambering out of the desk and sneaking out of the hall was out of the question. That fearsome headmistress, whose name I have expunged from my memory, would have been down on us like a ton of hairgrips – or whatever assemblage of hooks and pulleys she used to keep that formidable bun in place.

We were taught in classes of over 40, yet there weren't much more than 25 in the hall. Some were off with medical conditions (mumps and measles were rife at the time) and some had either not been put in for it or simply not turned up. So heaven knows what I was doing there. It was nothing to do with my parents. They didn't even seem aware that it was eleven-plus day. I'd simply told them that there was going to be some kind of test.

A writing test would have been the best description of the second paper, and my writing was barely legible. An examiner might have been able to read my name and where I lived. Not much more. I certainly couldn't do capitals or understand punctuation. The function of a full-stop was beyond my comprehension. Another hour seemed to stretch into infinity.

My joy was unbounded when I was eventually released into the playground and reunited with a football. Only when we went back into class and I heard other kids talking about the exam did I begin to feel a bit apprehensive.

Maybe my parents were starting to feel it too. Clearly other mothers had been talking about it because the first thing my Mum said when I got home was "Remember that test you took?"

"I couldn't really understand it," I shrugged.

She said "Don't worry; we'll get you a bike if you pass."

I think she knew in her heart of hearts that I wasn't going to do very well. Dad knew it too. "How did you do?" he asked after a quick briefing from Mum when he came home from work. And when I told him that I couldn't do it at all, he just said "Oh, don't worry; you'll be all right." Yes, he'd been to a grammar school, but it didn't seem to bother him that I wouldn't be following in father's footsteps. Like Mum, it seems that he just wanted me to be happy, in school and out of it. And I *was* happy most of the time, particularly with ball at feet or bat in hand, either in the playground or on our makeshift pitch behind the shops. That happiness was about to be cruelly curtailed, alas.

It was a couple of months or so after the exam, and school had broken up for the summer, when the envelope landed lightly on the doormat. All the same, I knew there was something weightily significant about it when my mother propelled me into the front parlour to open it – unprecedented on a weekday morning. Official confirmation that I'd failed the eleven plus made me feel second-rate and inadequate. All the more so when I discovered that most of the 25 or so who had been in that hall with me had passed, including most of my footballing friends.

Bradford apparently offered a larger percentage of grammar school places to its children than any other city in England. Had I known that at the time, I'd have felt even worse. Worse still, I would be shovelled into the C-stream at Wibsey Secondary Modern. You couldn't get much lower than that, even though my mother had assured me that "Wibsey's a lovely school and they play a lot of football".

Lovely?

We'd see about that come September. For now Mablethorpe beckoned. "We can't let you have that bike," Mum had told me, the tears welling as she said it, "but we will have a lovely holiday."

And we did. The unpredictable British weather was the only variable factor in our summer holidays. We'd set off from West Yorkshire to East Lincolnshire on the same train at the same time of year. It was Bradford holiday fortnight at the beginning of August when all the mills closed down. We were one of the few families on our estate that went for the full two weeks.

Always stayed at the same boarding house, needless to say. It was really what you might call a boarding bungalow, owned by a Mr and Mrs Holt who lived on site but let out a family room every week or fortnight. Mum and Dad had the double bed while Ann and I had camp beds almost at floor level. There was a "wireless" so that we could listen to the Light programme. No television, needless to say, and no telephone either.

Mr Holt spent most of his time in the garden, cultivating his own vegetables. It was at Mablethorpe that I sampled rhubarb and beetroot for the first time. There were Granny Smith's apples too and Mr Holt's runner beans made a pleasant change from stalky, soggy cabbage and lumpy Swede. Mind you, nobody could compete with my mother when it came to fish and chips.

"Rubbish" was her whispered verdict on Mrs Holt's attempts. The following week and every Mablethorpe Friday "dinnertime" thereafter, we'd buy fish and chips on the way back from the beach, eat them out of newspaper and ask for nothing more than a cup of tea when we reached the bungalow for our allotted one o'clock slot. Mrs Holt appeared mortally offended at first but she must have become used to it as the years passed.

On other days, that one o'clock lunch – or rather "dinner" – was served just over four and a half hours after the full-English breakfast had been seen off. With duck eggs. They were quite strongly flavoured with greenish yolks. Ann made a big fuss but I forced them down without too much complaint.

Coastal Lincolnshire seemed extraordinarily flat to a lad from Horton Bank Top. Great beach for cricket, mind you, and not so crowded as the vast and sandy wastelands of nearby Skegness. It was on this coast where, as Philip Larkin put it, "sky and Lincolnshire and water meet". "Eventually," he might have added. It was quite a trek to the frothing edge of the North Sea. Once you'd dipped in a toe, risking hypothermia in the process, you wondered why you'd bothered.

Very occasionally I'd take the plunge, knowing that

Mum would be waiting with a warm towel once I'd shivered my way through the marathon between the shore and the Kershaw windbreak. Then she'd persuade me to play with my little sister for half an hour. I'd dig a big hole and bury Ann up to her waist. Dad, meanwhile, was buried in his book while reclining in a deckchair. No change there. I'd then make a few sandcastles for Ann before being freed to find the nearest group of lads with a cricket bat. They'd usually be playing with a tennis ball at first. Not ideal with that sharp easterly breeze coming off the sea so, after a while, I'd suggest a hard, rubber ball. If I didn't have one with me, I could sometimes interrupt Dad's reading and persuade him to part with the cash which allowed me to scamper off to the nearby high street to buy one. As usual, I was under strict instructions not to venture into any of those amusement arcades on the way.

I wanted the holiday to go on forever. Particularly in that summer of uncertainty when Wibsey Secondary Modern School loomed on the autumnal horizon. Playing cricket behind the shops at Horton Bank Top was nowhere near as much fun as it had been in Mablethorpe. And not just because the surroundings were nowhere near as expansive.

Eleven minus

I was very conscious that most of my friends had passed to go to grammar school. So were they. Most of them wouldn't let me forget it. And slowly, but perhaps inevitably, that began to have an effect on me. Someone who'd always been comfortable in his own skin became quieter and more withdrawn.

That process began to speed up when term-time arrived and the differences between us became even more evident. They all had uniforms. I didn't. To some secondary-modern kids, a grammar-school cap was a target to be whipped off someone's head and thrown over a hedge. To me those caps and blazers were something to be envied. Seeing my once inseparable mates swaggering around in their uniforms had the effect of making me feel more and more like a loser. Slowly and perhaps inevitably, we grew apart. The sound of balls thumping against garage doors would soon become a distant echo of a happier past.

At least I kept in touch with my best friend Philip Lodge, if only through the church. To his immense credit, I never had the sense that he was looking down on me. Yet he had more claim than most to academic superiority, having made it to that most prestigious of local schools: Bradford Grammar. He would go on to read

English at Manchester University. But many years later, he still invited me to be best man at his wedding. He would have been best man at mine had he not been teaching English in Biafra at the time.

All that was a long way in the future back in 1953 as he set off sprightly for Bradford Grammar while I embarked on the two-mile trudge to Wibsey. The headmaster, one Frank Ball, made our former headmistress seem quite a kindly soul. He was a huge man with a bald head and a sadistic attachment to his cane. Mr Ball didn't just beat children; he seemed to relish leaving his mark on them – all too literally. Or so I was told by those unfortunate enough to be summoned to his office. I managed to escape with occasional "slipperings" from teachers for not working hard enough.

The head's assemblies were truly terrifying. The first one that I remember began with us all marching in behind our form teachers who stood at the side while we stood as erect and still as possible. Mr Ball started talking in a voice that seemed to bounce back off the walls and make the windows rattle. Then suddenly he stopped and paused for dramatic effect. Somebody along the row from me had twitched and smiled. "There's someone there who seems to think this is funny," Ball boomed. "Come to my room after assembly, boy. I'm going to cut the hide off you."

The kid burst into tears and slunk out of the room. I saw him afterwards, almost bent double with pain and said to him "You've got to tell your parents."

"Oh no," he said. "I'm not doing that. I'll get it again."

It was horrible. Ball did that on a regular basis – pick on a lad in assembly and give him a real thrashing. On one occasion I noticed my form teacher, Mr Smith, raise a disapproving eyebrow in the direction of a colleague. PE was his specialist subject and I excelled at that, if not much else. Apart from football and cricket, of course. I quickly became one of Mr Smith's acolytes. It was he who recommended me to Bradford Boys FC when I was about twelve. That gave me some status and, slowly but surely, began to restore some of my lost confidence.

Every Tuesday evening we used to go training at St Bede's, a Catholic grammar school, which had excellent sports facilities. In many parts of the country, of course, rugby was what grammar-school boys played. The round ball game was for the secondary modern "oiks". But rugby in Yorkshire meant rugby league, which didn't have the same social status as union. So the grammars dabbled with it but weren't over-keen, encouraging as it did sporting encounters with the wrong sort of person. Oh, the complexities of the British class system.

The following year, when I was spotted holding my own for Bradford Boys against ruffians from mining towns such as Barnsley and Castleford, I would sign schoolboy terms for Huddersfield Town FC. One of my team-mates there in the Northern Intermediate League casually told me that he'd passed the eleven plus but had declined the opportunity to go to grammar school. Why?

Because he'd have had to play rugby union.

He was rather good at the round-ball game and wanted to stick with it. I could soon see why. A fisherman's son from Aberdeen, he was the youngest of seven children brought up in a council flat. But when it came to football, he was what the pundits call "different class".

His name was Denis Law.

CHAPTER THREE

Damned with faint praise

It was "40 years on", as they used to sing at Eton but not at Bradford secondary moderns. I was back in the headmaster's office that I'd come to know so well. Different head-teacher, of course. Different school from Wibsey too. There'd been a reorganisation of secondary education in Bradford at the end of my second year, as we used to call it. As a result, a brand new secondary modern had opened its doors and I was only too grateful to walk through them.

Buttershaw was only a mile away from home, closer than Wibsey and far less crowded insofar as it had been built for 1,000 pupils yet only 360 had been admitted. So far. Plenty of space then as well as an abundance of brand new facilities. We even had a uniform. Green blazer with a big red badge, gleaming white shirt, grey socks and grey flannels. Short grey flannels, I might add, which must have looked ridiculous on a big lad like me. Still, I felt slightly more comfortable on those occasions when I bumped into former friends who were now grammar-school boys. Life was getting better.

Thanks Shanks

The head-teacher was much more civilised than the bawling Mr Ball with his ever-present threat of a thrashing. Mr Cook didn't believe in corporal punishment. He'd come from a grammar school but was a firm advocate of comprehensive education. And, yes, Buttershaw did eventually become a comprehensive. Not in my time, however. Oh, no.

Still, the teachers took an interest. For the first time in my life I was given specific help with English. Slowly but surely, I began to understand sentences and paragraphs. Just as well. Apart from anything else, I was given homework. I'd go back to my little box-room and sit on the bed with an exercise book on my lap. (No room for a desk in there.) The subject that I enjoyed most was geography and, eventually, I began to scratch out essays of a sort on subjects such as the Yorkshire woollen industry.

My reading was also starting to improve. Instead of just looking at pictures of the two Stans, Matthews and Mortensen, I could move a finger slowly along each line of my football magazine and find out a bit about those stars of the unforgettable Cup Final of 1953. Before long I was browsing through the sports pages of the Telegraph and Argus every evening. It was a way of keeping up with affairs at Bradford Park Avenue since I could only go to floodlit evening matches with my Dad. On Saturday afternoons I was usually otherwise engaged, playing football for Bradford Boys in the winter or cricket in the summer months.

Apart opening the batting and keeping wicket for the school team, I was also playing for Wibsey Congs CC. "Congs" was short for Congregational, the church with which the club was no longer connected. We played in the Bradford Central League, no less, one division below the Bradford League, to which I would eventually ascend after a toughening up process that was the norm in the Yorkshire form of what was laughably called a "gentlemen's game".

For all my improvements in reading, I was nowhere near ready to embark on hefty tomes by Dickens or Robert Louis Stevenson, let alone Shakespeare's sonnets. Science, meanwhile, remained a mystery. As for maths lessons, they were a complete no-go.

From the age of thirteen (and a half), I had the perfect excuse for missing maths. I could claim to be on head-boy duties. Mr Cook had appointed me to that role at a comparatively early age. Partly, I suspect, because he thought that I was a "nice lad" – he said as much to my

Mum one fateful day, albeit with a somewhat damning caveat – and partly because I had size and presence. I was not only captain of the school football team but had also been selected to play for a select eleven representing schools through the whole city. That gained me some grudging respect from not-so-nice lads who could all too easily have challenged my authority as head-boy. And that respect grew when Huddersfield Town came a-calling while I was still at Buttershaw.

I also seemed to attract some brazen flirtation from certain shameless girls. Yet when it came to the opposite sex, I was hopeless. Still very much a Mummy's boy. I remained embarrassed and tongue-tied whenever a girl "came on to me", as today's youngsters would put it. It would take a few years before that began to change and, by that time, I'd long left school.

As head-boy, I spent quite a bit of time in Mr Cook's office – the same office to which I would return . . . was it really 40 years on? More like 46. No wonder so many memories flooded back. It was there that head-teacher and head-boy had devised a scheme worthy of Dick Barton, Special Agent, to expose an outbreak of thieving from the changing rooms. When the culprit was finally exposed, Mr Cook didn't do what Mr Ball would have done and "cut the hide" off him. Instead he called the parents in and told them "Look, this is a criminal offence and, if it happens again, I'll have to tell the police."

That sort of approach was very enlightened for the time. Mr Cook was widely admired by progressive educationalists. I noticed that and watched carefully as he welcomed visitors to Bradford's newest school. Before long, I was showing them around in my capacity as head-boy. Some of them seemed impressed. For all my educational drawbacks, I was learning how to put on a show.

My self-confidence was growing – and for once it wasn't confined to the sports field. Then along came something sharp and jolting to hack it back as effectively as well-oiled shears. The one wielding them was someone who had my best interests at heart and evidently believed that a judicious trim would eventually lead to healthier growth at a later stage.

I was fourteen (and three quarters) when Mr Cook called me once again into the office with which I'd become quite familiar. On this occasion, however, he also called in my mother who wasn't familiar with it at all. Neither of my parents had ever gone anywhere near any of my schools. This, I sensed, was something serious. And this is what he said:

"Your son is a lovely lad. He's a wonderful head- boy and he'll have to leave in a few months time, when he's fifteen. But I can get him a job now that will set him up in a real trade."

What would that job be? An apprenticeship at a printer's called Wilson's of Wibsey, apparently. It was all too evident that Mr Cook didn't expect me to take any exams, even though they were only CSEs – Certificate of Secondary Education, since you ask, and for "Secondary" read second-rate. At the grammar schools they took the qualification that employers, colleges and universities took seriously: GCEs or, to give them their full title, General Certificates of Education.

Sssshhh. The head was talking again. "As I said, Mrs Kershaw, David's a very nice lad and good with people. *But he's not very bright.*"

Those words will be with me 'til the day I die. Particularly the last five words, almost said as an afterthought. They came back to me forcibly when I walked back into that office in 2002 as an adviser employed by the Department of Education. By that time I'd been a head-teacher myself for 21 years. A successful one, too. If that sounds a bit self-aggrandising then I'm sorry. "You've shown 'em" were the words that came to mind as I looked out of the same window over the same car park adjoining the same school hall. There were a lot more cars, of course, and they were very different from the Morris Minors, Austin A35s and Ford Populars of the 1950s. The furnishings in here had changed too, but the room was still the same size and I was still waiting for the head-teacher to make an appearance.

Not Mr Cook, needless to say, although I'd wished that it had been – if only for the opportunity to tell him that, however progressive you think you are, you don't write kids off at 14 as "not very bright". Here I was, sitting in the office where the man for whom I'd had such respect had uttered those words that could have wrecked my life. It hadn't, thanks to the intervention of an inspirational football manager who was prepared to put his money where his perception was. Throughout my career in education, I'd been driven by a belief that any youngster at any time can make improvements and, irrespective of background or abilities, they can make a contribution.

Suddenly the head-teacher's secretary interrupted my reverie by peering around the door and enquiring "Would you like a cup of coffee?" before adding "He won't be long."

The "he" in this case was the head I'd come to see. Can't remember his name now but I do remember that too many Bradford schools had been declared inadequate by Ofsted and responsibility for education had been taken out of local authority hands. In this case there'd been a complaint by a student's parents that his misconduct had been mishandled and he'd been sworn at. The boy, that is, by the head who was understandably anxious and therefore potentially aggressive when he finally turned up. But his attitude changed very quickly when I said "Look, I'm here as a professional colleague who happens to have a history in this place. I want to help you to do the right thing by that student."

Then I went to see the parents who accepted his explanation that there'd been a misunderstanding by their son and he hadn't really sworn at all. It was something about nothing, as it turned out. But at least it had given me chance to take a glimpse into my past and reflect on the long journey away from it.

It had also brought back the conversation with my mother after we'd walked home from that meeting with Mr Cook. Suddenly I stopped and blurted out "I don't want to be a printer at Wilson's, Mum. I'm going to get myself a job where *I* want to work." That may have been because I was already resenting what the head had said. Or it may have been because I didn't want to come home covered in ink. Instead I wanted an office job, like my Dad, while I pursued the ultimate dream of becoming a professional footballer.

So I started straying away from the sports pages in the Telegraph and Argus and into the "small ads". It was there that I read that an audit assistant was required in the town hall at Morley, near Leeds. Bear in mind that I couldn't do maths to save my life, although I could add up. Just about. Anyway, I managed to fill in the application form well enough to be called in for an interview. And, lo and behold, somehow I landed the job. The pay was £6 a week, but I was also getting another fiver for turning out every Saturday with other teenagers who were on the books at Huddersfield Town. Okay, I had to give my mother half of all that. Still, £5 and 10 shillings (£5.50) in your back pocket every seven days wasn't bad for a 14-year-old in those days. Bear in mind that I was paid only £9 a week when I finally started teaching after three years at college. Needless to say, that was still some way in the future.

At Morley Town Hall I was basically an office boy,

clearing up and making tea. But I did have to tick off and sign the dustmen's worksheets. The smell of those wretched log books stayed with me for years. More fragrant by far were the "young ladies" in our office. There were five or six of them, all older than me. But there were a couple in their early 20s and, in the summer months, they'd ask me to come with them to a nearby bowling green every lunchtime. Being Yorkshire, it was crown green bowls and, being me, I was still a bit tongue-tied. Not exactly Errol Flynn or David Niven. Two older colleagues were better at chat-up lines between launching their bowls over that deceptively uneven green. Slowly but surely, mind you, I was beginning to relax in female company and recognise women as proper, lovely human beings.

Not something I could ever have said about the City Treasurer, one Jasper Jennings – a classic local-authority bureaucrat if ever there was one. National president of the Institute of Municipal Treasurers and Accountants, no less, and he certainly looked the part. He was always immaculately dressed, from his stiff white collar to his shiny black shoes. Even sported one of those gold watch chains across his waistcoat, in the manner of northern aldermen.

One day he stopped me in the corridor and said "You've got no qualifications, have you?"

I nodded to confirm that his assumption was correct, and kept my head down as a matter of shame.

"Well, you ought to try to get some."

"Right," I responded, looking up and meeting him squarely in the eye. "I will."

And I did. Eventually. Professional football was beckoning alluringly in the meantime. I'd been on Huddersfield's books from the age of 13 and the dream of becoming a pro' seemed almost touchable. Little did I know, as that dream came close to reality, that it would be the making of me. Not as a celebrated centre-half, alas. Nor as an accountant. Not in my wildest dreams could I have imagined that football would provide me with the means to enter a career that would prove to be far more fulfilling in the long run.

Thanks Shanks

CHAPTER FOUR

Steak'n'chips'n' Roker Park

My all-too-brief introduction to professional football had begun a year or two earlier when I was still at school and two strange men turned up on the touchline. They were an odd couple, to put it mildly. One looked like a private investigator or a tabloid journalist. He wore an enormous overcoat with the collar pulled up. The other had cropped hair and sported old-fashioned football boots with big bulbous caps over the toes. Between his shaved 'napper' and what you might call his hob-nailed studs was an equally old-fashioned tracksuit made of wool. Well, we were in Bradford. On the playing fields at St Bede's Catholic Grammar School, to be precise. As I mentioned in an earlier chapter, St Bede's had the best pitches in the city, providing an appropriate home ground for the select XI known as Bradford Boys.

The odd couple turned out to be representatives of Huddersfield Town's under-18 side, which played in the Northern Intermediate League. The one in the overcoat was the scout; the one in the tracksuit the coach, Eddie Boot, formerly a distinguished wing-half who had played for the club in the 1938 FA Cup Final and taken over the captaincy in the post-war years. Until 1952, that is, when he'd hung up his boots – his playing boots anyway.

Eddie would eventually take over the management of the first team after the all-too-brief reign of Bill Shankly. But that was four years away yet. His raucous voice, laced by language best described as "industrial", would become part of the soundtrack of my life in the meantime.

For now he was quietly spoken and polite. He and the scout had seemed to step out of nowhere. I hadn't been remotely aware of their presence while the game was in progress.

"Are your parents here?" one of them asked.

"No," I replied, slightly baffled and increasingly nervous.

"Do you mind if we come and see them?"

"Why?"

"Well, you had a good game today. Do you like tackling like that?"

"I do."

"Thought so. We want to talk to your Mum and Dad

about the possibility of you becoming a footballer. A proper footballer."

When they told me that they were from Huddersfield, I was astounded and absolutely overjoyed. No, it wasn't Bradford Park Avenue, but this was 1955 and Town were back in the top flight and had reached the quarter finals of the FA Cup. They were a club with a proud history. Won the League three times in three successive seasons in the 1920s under one Herbert Chapman, who went on to make an even bigger name for himself at Arsenal.

I rushed home to tell my mother that two men wanted to come and see her. "Dad too."

First question: "Have you done anything wrong?"

On the contrary, I assured her. I'd done something right. Played well enough to get myself noticed by representatives of a First Division football club.

Next question: "When are they coming?"

The front parlour was duly polished until every surface seemed to gleam. Out came the best china. And home came Dad who beamed proudly at me as he shut the door and discussions began. I was on the other side of the door and, no, I couldn't really hear what was being said.

So I retreated to the kitchen and glowed in the

warmth of the range. Walking those few yards from the parlour was almost a road-to-Damascus experience. My life's going to change so much for the better, I thought to myself. Okay, I'm no good at maths and not much better at anything else when it comes to school work. But when it comes to football, these guys wouldn't be here if they didn't think I had something.

The deal was duly done. In return for my fiver a week, I would be expected to turn out for training on three evenings as well as for matches every Saturday morning. We were one step down from the reserves and weren't allowed to play on the hallowed first-team pitch at Leeds Road in Huddersfield. Yet, funnily enough, we did play on the equivalents at Leeds United's Elland Road, Sheffield Wednesday's Hillsborough and Sunderland's Roker Park, where vast empty terraces echoed with the bellows of Eddie Boot. There were very few others present.

And we were allowed to go to Town on certain Saturday afternoons, to watch if not to play. We were given free tickets for first-team home games after each match at our ground at Cleckheaton, which was about eight miles and two bus journeys from Horton Bank Top.

Leeds Road was another 20 minutes from Cleckheaton

on yet another bus. But it was well worth the trip to stand behind the dug-out and watch the likes of Jimmy Glazzard who'd been playing for Town for the best part of 10 years. Jimmy was a much-loved centre-forward of the old-school with a tendency to hang in the air and head improbable goals. Not quite as high or for quite as long as the Scot who'd soon be heading (all too literally) for Huddersfield, but he was a young shaver who just happened to be a footballing phenomenon. Glazzard was coming to the end of his career and I used to stand there on the terraces working out how I'd tackle him. Perhaps because he was slowing down, he was becoming frustrated and leaving his mark on his markers. Many a centre-half would retaliate and find that they were the ones being sent off. It just confirmed my belief in tackling hard but keeping cool.

Admittedly I took less notice of a young left-back who had returned from National Service and made his debut against Manchester United in 1955. He would thrive during Bill Shankly's time at Leeds Road and go on to play for England on no fewer than 63 occasions, including a rather important match against West Germany in 1966. By that time, however, he had signed for Everton.

Ray Wilson no longer remembers playing for England

on the only occasion that the country that gave football to the world won the World Cup. He suffers from Alzheimer's disease, and he's hardly alone in that among footballers from that era.

As I knew all too well, heading those heavy, wet leather case balls could sometimes make you feel as though you'd just been coshed. It hurt even more if the seam hit you full on. But there was no backing away from it. Particularly if you were a centre-forward or a centre-half, as I was, it was your job to meet the ball full on. Preferably with your forehead.

My career as a pro' came to an end all too soon and, at the time, it seemed as though my world had ended too. It may have been the end of my brain, however, had I 'enjoyed' a full career in a game that increased in speed and intensity the further you stepped up the ladder.

The step up from Bradford Boys to Huddersfield Town under-18s was noticeable enough, insofar as everything – not just the crosses and the corners – happened quicker. You had to learn quickly, to control quickly and to pass quickly. There was no time on the ball. The centre-forwards I came up against were as tough as the ones I'd played against in the mining towns, but faster and more skilful.

Steak'n'chips'n' Roker Park

There was an awful lot of aggression. Uncompromis-ing sliding tackles were the norm. They were also my speciality. So, yes, I was threatened with retaliation all the time, but I just smiled and turned away. That was the Sunday school Methodist in me, following the example of Jesus and turning the other cheek. Nobody ever got up and thumped me or even threw a punch at my back. That may have been because I was still bigger than anyone else on the field. I was always pulling other players apart, telling them to calm down.

The swearing never stopped, on the field and off. My team-mates and the opposition would break up syllables to insert the F-word. Once in the dressing room, they'd go on and on about women, giving them marks out of 10 in terms of their looks, their shape or their size. It was low-level chauvinistic nastiness. Bravado, too, in most cases. The majority of the team were 14 or 15.

I didn't join in these conversations because I was never what you might call "one of the lads". On the other hand, I wasn't alienated or picked on. Perhaps that was because of my size or my tackling or my interventions in potential punch-ups. I remember walking out on to the pitch for one game and one of the lads coming up to me. "David," he said – nobody ever called me 'Dave' – "are you all right?"

"I'm fine," I said.

"You never join in, do you?" he went on.

"I don't say much," I shrugged. "All this dirty talk's just not me."

"Okay, that's great," he said. And we both ran off to take up our positions.

On Saturday mornings I used to have to get up at 5.30 and catch the bus into the city centre. The one to Cleckheaton left from outside the Town Hall. In those days most men worked on Saturdays, until "dinnertime" at least. Many of them were miners or mill-workers, off to do a shift. If there were no seats downstairs, I'd go up to the top deck and grope my way through a fug of cigarette smoke. You could see the nicotine clinging to the ceiling.

Many of my fellow passengers were coughing and wheezing but, in quite a few cases, that may have had as much to do with the coal dust as the smoke in their lungs. Those journeys gave me time to reflect on the miserable lives that so many of my contemporaries were enduring. It made me even more determined to make something of my own life. No, footballers didn't earn much more than factory workers at the time. At least, though, there was an aura about earning a living through sport. For one thing, it gave you the chance to get away from your surroundings at regular intervals and travel to other parts of the country – by private coach rather than smoke-infested public transport.

At our level, admittedly, the journeys were fairly parochial. We rarely ventured outside Yorkshire. London was another land and even Manchester was the other side of the Pennine fortress. The furthest we travelled was to Weirside. Those trips to Roker Park were memorable, and not just because I had to get up even earlier to make sure that I was on that coach from Cleckheaton.

We stopped on the way at the historic town of Ripon with its cathedral and market place. It seemed out of this world. Certainly out of my world. What's more, we went into a hotel for the first time in my life and, I suspect, for the first time in the lives of my team-mates. I can't remember the name of it now, and I suppose it was really a posh pub with rooms. Needless to say, most of "the lads" were clamouring for a pint.

No chance. It was soft drinks only. But there was also food, the main reason for stopping there. We had sandwiches on the way and, believe it or not, steak and chips on the way back. Much better than brisket, that's for sure. I'd never tasted anything like it. Tucking it away beneath those beams and horse brasses amounted to an experience that that made me feel a very long way from our kitchen and even further from the chip shop where Mum had taught Harry Ramsden how to batter haddock. To me it seemed like a world of wealth and star quality.

Stars on the football field were in short supply at our level. But that was about to change. Stardom would arrive in the form of an unlikely incomer from somewhere even further north than Sunderland.

CHAPTER FIVE

Great Scots at Cleckheaton

Before the arrival of "the boy", sightings of the Huddersfield first-team manager Andy Beattie at Cleckheaton were about as rare as willow warblers on Horton Bank Top. We were one league below the reserves and therefore unworthy of his gaze – unless, that is, his attention was drawn to a particularly prodigious talent.

It was Beattie who signed 15-year-old Denis Law in April 1956, after being tipped off by his brother Archie, a scout for the club in their native Scotland. "The boy's a freak," [Andy] Beattie proclaimed. "Never did I see a less likely football prospect – weak, puny and bespectacled."

The functional NHS specs didn't last long as his squint was quickly corrected by an operation. But, my goodness, he was small – ridiculously so to someone of my size. "For goodness sake," I muttered under my breath when I first peered down on this short, pale and skinny kid who just happened to be older than me.

Then I saw what he could do with a football and my contempt quickly turned to awe. He could control it in an instant, on his instep, on his knee or on his chest, whatever speed it came towards him. As for his movement, it was so smooth and so fast.

I later discovered that he had worn canvas plimsolls in all weathers until he was twelve and handed-down shoes thereafter. His first football boots were second-hand, a birthday present from a neighbour in their tenement in a poor part of Aberdeen, who evidently recognised that this boy stood out from the clamorous clan of street footballers outside his window. Denis was the youngest of four boys and had three older sisters. He didn't see much of his father, George, who was fighting with the Royal Navy for the first five years of his life. He'd survived the Second World War as well as the First, when he'd been shot in the leg while serving in the army. Now George Law relied on fishing to earn a living and was away for days on end. Pickings were evidently meagre from that chilly and choppy North Sea that would later become a rich and plentiful supplier of oil.

The train journey south to Huddersfield took about as long as a jet plane today would take to fly half way around the world. Young Denis must have felt incredibly homesick to be far away from his family in what was, to him, another country in another world. In fact, he later admitted as much in his autobiography, The King, published by Bantam Books in 2003.

But that wasn't the kind of thing that you talked about in the dressing room. The Scottish whiz-kid quickly became one of the lads. He did his fair share of effing and blinding but, for the most part, he exuded a quiet confidence. And that grew as he grew. Slightly taller, that is; he never put on much weight.

On one occasion he casually dropped out in conversation that he'd turned down a chance to go to Aberdeen Grammar School. Yes, it was because they played rugby rather than "proper football". The other lads nodded sagely, as though they'd have done exactly the same in the circumstances. But somehow it rankled with me. Deep down I'd never quite got over being such an abject failure at the eleven-plus.

News about the phenomenal talent that had arrived at Cleckheaton spread quickly. It wasn't just Andy Beattie who was making unaccustomed appearances on our touchline. Readers of that esteemed organ, the Huddersfield Examiner, were turning up in some numbers to see what all the fuss was about.

They soon found out. Like me, they would never forget the first time that they saw Denis leap to meet a corner.

He was far shorter than the opposition's centre-half, but he just soared above him and seemed to hover there. Suddenly the ball bulleted into the back of the net. There were gasps on the touchline and a general outburst from the other players which amounted, in many cases, to "foooooocking hell". The "weak" "freak" from Scotland had just made Jimmy Glazzard, long-time hero of many a Huddersfield fan, seem like a man with weights in his boots.

As a centre-half myself, it made me extremely grateful that Denis was on our side. Mind you, his presence soon led to me being given an additional role as his personal bodyguard on the field. Our coach had confided "He's a marked lad is Denis." (Everybody was "a lad" to Eddie Boot.) I soon saw what he meant and I was honoured to do as I was bid and play my part in protecting him from the "cloggers" who would be doing their best to stifle his wizardry at every opportunity.

Not surprisingly, young Law didn't like being pushed around and he'd sometimes hit back. And not surprisingly either, he didn't pose much of a threat to the cloggers. They just brushed him off. I distinctly remember playing the Sheffield Wednesday side at Hillsborough and, as we walked off at half-time, I went over the two players who'd knocked him for six. "If you do that again," I growled, "I'll come and sort you out."

"Oh, right. We'll see, won't we," was the all too predictable response.

With Eddie Boot's permission, I played slightly out of position for the first ten minutes of the second half and bided my time. Eventually one of the cloggers approached with the ball at his feet. In I went. Didn't punch him, of course; I just tackled him in a way that hit him for six. What's more, the ref didn't give a foul. Nobody touched Denis again in that game.

He didn't say anything about it during or after that match but there were a couple of times when he showed his appreciation by coming over at full time and admitting "I'm glad you were there today." Denis, needless to say, would be here today and gone tomorrow as far as the Northern Intermediate League was concerned.

Aged 16 and 303 days, he made his first-team debut against Notts County at Meadow Lane on Christmas Eve, 1956. And he scored a goal for the first time for the first team when County came to Town at Leeds Road on the Boxing Day. It wouldn't be the last.

Beattie had resigned the previous month, having

failed to stop relegation to Division Two six months earlier. His replacement all too quickly made his presence felt throughout the club. Bill Shankly wasn't going to risk playing Law against grown men, week in, week out, so his inherited protégé would return for outings at Cleckheaton on a fairly regular basis. When he turned out, the crowds turned up and The Boss would be among them.

Shankly came from a small Ayrshire mining village that produced a disproportionate number of professional footballers, most of them desperate to get out of the pits and out of poverty. All four of his brothers made it as pro's. Had they all been at their peak at the same time, they would have made a formidable five-a-side team.

As it turned out, only one became a household name, south as well as north of the border. "Bill" – not that I'd have dared to call him that – had an aura about him. His every word seemed to count. At the end of a game, he wouldn't just disappear. He'd come into our dressing room and sum it up. "Now," he might say, "I saw on three occasions somebody miss or not recover quickly enough, leaving a space from which they could have scored. If you miss a tackle or find yourself out of position, you roll up your sleeves and you get back. I don't want any of you feeling sorry for yourselves."

That's the abridged version, minus the 'f' word with which Shankly punctuated his utterances at fairly regular intervals. But you didn't laugh it off or think to yourself "Who's this silly old sod?" This bloke had got something.

One of his philosophies about football was that it was a collective thing. You didn't play for yourself; you worked for each other. Looking back on it now, I can see that he had old-fashioned co-operative values that almost certainly came from his background in a mining community. And he'd quickly imparted his philosophy to Eddie Boot, which explained why I was called upon to protect Denis Law on the field. Even that star-in-the-making wouldn't be allowed to swagger. Shankly took great pleasure in keeping players' feet on the ground. Not literally in Denis's case, of course. The manager valued his ability to jump and hover as much as anybody and probably more than most.

We looked on Shankly like a god. Suddenly, it seemed, we were entering a new era and I felt confident that I would be part of it. So much so that I handed in my notice at Morley Town Hall, without having heeded Jasper Jennings's advice about getting some qualifications. I wouldn't miss the smell of those dustmen's worksheets.

What would be more difficult to confine to the past were those lunchtime games of crown-green bowls with fragrant young ladies. But football was the future and the future looked bright.

Until the end of April, 1959, that is. It was the last game of the season. Contracts were up for renewal. Law's was assured, of course, but he was making one of his increasingly rare appearances in our league. Like the rest of us, he would have been well aware that the Boss was there, making assessments of a squad that might – just might – provide him with another prospect or two.

I can't remember who we were playing but the ref was already looking at his watch when I missed a vital tackle. Their centre-forward went through and scored. Two-one to them. End of the game. End of my dreams.

Law came over and kicked me in the shins. Not too hard, to be honest, and, yes, I still had my shin-pads on. "You've just cost me five quid," he snapped. That was his win bonus. Much higher than anybody else in the team, needless to say. He was a professional already, fiercely competitive and committed to winning every match, even at this level.

I could have threatened him. I could have flattened him. But I did neither. Being me, I just shrugged and walked away, back to my peg in that tip of a dressing room. There were no lockers. The toilets stank. The place was soon strewn with dirty socks, shirts and shorts. Not to mention discarded jockstraps. Even the communal bath was all-too-quickly scummed with mud steamed from the knees of sweaty adolescents cracking crude jokes and singing filthy songs.

I stayed just long enough to get clean. Having emerged and grabbed my towel, I was heading back to my part of the dressing room when I was stopped dead by what seemed like a very cold hand on my still-warm shoulder.

"David," growled an all-too-familiar Scottish voice, "just come away here." Mr Shankly led the way to a bench well away from the still-raucous wallowers in the communal bath. The Boss came straight to the point. "Look, David," he said. "I've made up my mind. You're a great lad, but you're not quite quick enough."

Now where had I heard that before? Or something like it. "David's a very nice lad, Mrs Kershaw, and good with people. But he's not very bright." The parting words of that "progressive" head-teacher Mr Cook came back to haunt me. Not that they'd ever really gone away.

So that was it. I was not quick enough to be a professional footballer and not bright enough to be anything else. Or so I was thinking to myself as that abrasive Ayrshire accent sliced through the noise from the bath once more. "I need to talk to you properly," Shankly went on. "Come and see me in my office on Monday morning and I'll get you a job."

And with that he walked off to talk to somebody else who had just emerged from the murky steam. I just sat there, head down and elbows on the knees protruding from my towel while trying to contemplate what lay ahead. First there was the long and grinding road back to Horton Bank Top. At least I was no longer reliant on the buses, having bought myself a Lambretta motor scooter soon after my 16th birthday. Come Monday morning, there would be an even longer journey to Huddersfield. And in between there would be a seemingly endless 24 hours that would make a normal Sunday in 1950s Bradford seem positively festive by comparison.

CHAPTER SIX

Saturday night and Sunday yawning

It was round about one o'clock on that fateful Saturday and Denis Law had already left the changing room. He may have been deprived of his win bonus by my last-minute missed tackle, but he still had the world at his feet and wasn't going to hang around amid the detritus of the Northern Intermediate League any longer than he had to. Bill Shankly, meanwhile, was still doing the rounds, patting some of the lads on the back and sitting down with others to tell them that, like me, they weren't going to make it.

Having finally roused myself from being bent almost double in disbelief, I'd dressed quickly. I just wanted to get out. Not that I was remotely hungry, despite having played 90 minutes of hard and fast football. Instead of heading for the canteen, I strode briskly towards the Lambretta. With one gloved hand gripping the throttle and the other the clutch, I glanced back at the dressing room, still strewn with filthy socks and filthy shirts, still ringing with filthy songs and filthy jokes, still harbouring a filthy bath and filthy toilets.

Thanks Shanks

No, I wasn't going to miss it. What I was going to miss was pitting myself against some of the best young footballers in Yorkshire and Wearside. I was going to miss steak and chips on the way back from Roker Park. But most of all I was going to miss the dream of moving onwards and upwards to something bigger and better.

Whether my team-mates were going to miss me I'd never know. All I'd done was shout "cheerio" from the doorway. I wasn't going to talk to anyone about what had just happened. That wasn't my style. You didn't show your emotions. Particularly in Yorkshire in the 1950s.

Deep down inside, though, I was in turmoil. As I slowly opened that clutch, I felt as though I was letting go of my future – the future that I had long imagined for myself as a professional footballer playing on famous grounds in front of huge crowds. All my insecurities came flooding back. I felt again that I was useless, worthless. The complimentary things that people in authority had said about me – that I was a nice lad and good with people – just disappeared. The rest of the weekend was yawning away into emptiness. So, it seemed, was the rest of my life.

The nigh-on 15-mile journey home ended with the Lambretta groaning its way up to Horton Bank Top and coming to a welcome halt outside our house. It was time to tell my parents.

Dad wasn't there. I should have known that. He was a man of regular habits and, at that time on a Saturday, he would be heading for Bradford Park Avenue to meet his mates for an end-of-season game. But I still had to tell my Mum. Having reassured her that Mr Shankly was going to get me a job, she simply said "Don't worry about the football. You'll be all right. We'll look after you."

My sister was out with her mates. No change there. Ann spent as little time at home as possible. Mum didn't treat her half as well as she treated me, the golden boy. I was the lucky one who felt part of a loving family. But I didn't feel lucky on this, the bleakest of Saturdays.

I just went upstairs to my box-room, sat on the end of the single bed that almost filled it, gazed out of the window and moped. Beyond the houses across the road, sheep were grazing on the hills that faced towards Halifax. Quite a pleasant view, I suppose. There are probably people of my age still living on the Cooperville estate and telling incomers "It was all fields round here in my day."

Me? I just took it for granted. Those ancient hills could have been belching mills for all I cared as visions of that dapper chap, Jasper Jennings, obliterated the sheep. The City Treasurer was looking at me sternly, a thumb in each waistcoat pocket, either side of that aldermanic watch chain. "I told you to get some qualifications," he kept saying over and over again.

Dad didn't say anything when he came home from the match. Mum would have told him about the end of my football contract as soon as he came through the door. But he always evaded difficult domestic discussions if at all possible. When I came down to get something to eat, he was buried in the sporting "Pink", probably reading about the game that he'd just witnessed. All cities of any size had football papers in those days, printed either on pink, blue or green paper. Bradford was no exception. They were rushed out early on Saturday evenings and, if there was a long bus queue outside the ground, someone could well be selling copies as soon as you alighted in the city centre.

On this occasion the paper provided Dad with a barrier to any man-to-man conversation with his son about what the hell he was going to do with the rest of his life. When I came back from the kitchen, his armchair was empty, offering me the opportunity to pinch the Pink and nip back upstairs with it. Reading about that afternoon's game at Park Avenue in my slow and laboured way at least allowed me to forget about Huddersfield Town for a while.

Saturday evening was card-game night at our house and the routine was as regular as clockwork. My parents' friends would arrive around six-ish and play would commence at 6.30 prompt. Sandwiches would be served at 7.30 and everybody would go home at 10. There would be men present, unlike on Thursdays when the front parlour was full of the giggles and gossip of Mum's friends only, and Dad made himself scarce. On Saturday evenings he organised the games – gin rummy, for the most part, but without any gin. I never saw a bottle of alcohol in our house. There was no shortage of cigarettes, mind you. All adults seemed to smoke in those days. When I finally came downstairs again and peered into the hallowed sanctuary of the parlour, it was as though a thick fog had descended on our front room.

Somewhere in there I could hear the booming voice of Uncle Eric. But it was Auntie Renee who spotted me and called me over to sit by her on the settee. No, we weren't related but all our parents' friends expected to be addressed as either Auntie or Uncle. Auntie Renee was a single woman and maybe she yearned for a son of her own. She was always very kind to me and, on this occasion, she immediately sensed that I was not myself. "David," she said, as soon as I slumped down behind her card hand, "what's the matter?"

"Oh nothing," I shrugged. "I've just had a bad day."

"Don't worry, you'll be all right," she assured me, patting me on the knee and sounding very like my mum. Come to think of it, Mum may well have told her about Shankly's assessment of my lack of prospects as a professional footballer.

Much as I liked Auntie Renee, I didn't want to go into details about what had happened . . . was it only seven or eight hours ago? So slow was the passage of time that weekend that it seemed more like seven or eight days.

As the adults embarked on another hand of rummy, I slipped away through the fog of fag smoke and headed back up to my room. I threw myself on the bed, buried my head in the pillow and cried. Just sobbed. Heaven knows what my former team-mates and opposing centre forwards would have made of that. Big, teak-tough David, defender of Denis Law, fearless tackler, respected intervener in many a confrontation – and here he was, crying like a girl. Eventually I must have fallen into a fitful sleep, waking at regular intervals and savouring that brief moment of consciousness before bad memories of the previous day came rushing back.

Sunday morning dawned. Eventually. I must have looked rather tired and red-eyed but nobody said anything over breakfast or, indeed, at Cooperville Methodist Church. The service started at 10.30. A bloke called Brian Wilson started playing the old pipe organ in a manner somewhat different from his namesake, the keyboard whizz-kid of the Beachboys, whose California Sound would be crackling through Radio Luxembourg in a few years time.

No, this Brian's speciality was hymns. There were four or five of them interspersed through a non-conformist service that included a sermon and a few prayers. And, no, I didn't send up any private prayers asking God to help me. Unlike Denis, I obviously would never have any God-given talent. Not enough of it anyway.

This was one of those occasions when I felt no engagement with the on-going service. Outside in the fresh air again, I chatted to old mates from the days when we booted balls against the garages behind the shop. Grammar-school boys for the most part, including my best friend Philip who went to the best school of all and evidently had a glittering future ahead of him.

Thanks Shanks

Did I tell him, or them, about the end of my footballing dreams?

"Did I hell as like," as we used to say in Bradford. They'd find out soon enough. For now I wanted to keep what status I had as a budding pro'. But that sense of failure and shame came flooding back as I said farewell to Philip and headed home for dinner. Brisket would be served at one o'clock sharp. A small slice for my sister and me, needless to say, albeit with "Yorkshires" that ballooned despite being flooded with gravy. You could almost imagine the air escaping from them with the first prod of the fork.

Ann shovelled hers down as quickly as possible before heading off up the road to her friends, the Dinsdales. Mum made a few attempts at conversation. Dad said very little. No reference was made to what had happened the previous day and what lay ahead on Monday morning at Leeds Road.

Still to be endured between now and then was the yawning emptiness of Sunday afternoon. My days at Sunday school were over by then so I was condemned to spend even longer than usual in the front parlour. There were two armchairs and a settee in there. All were built to last and had very wide arms. My Dad sat in one armchair and I slumped in the other. His snores were soon drowning out what passed for comedy in programmes such as Meet the Huggetts on the Light Programme. Despite the racket he was making, I found myself slipping into a doze, as though I'd had a few pints as well as a roast dinner. Needles to say, I hadn't. All I could put it down to was lack of sleep. Dwelling on the recent past and mithering about an uncertain future is not a gateway to restfulness and sweet dreams. Especially on a pillow made damp by tears.

At least dozing helped to pass the time. Every now and then I'd wake up to see Mum doing the ironing, serenaded by the wireless. I was neither braced by brass bands nor soothed by crooners. Once again I slept fitfully. Don't even recall being cheered by the intrusion of Dick Barton, Special Agent. Or maybe he was on after tea, for which we would adjourn to the kitchen-diner at five o'clock precisely. Crusty bread was spread with butter that came from the grocer's in wrapped slabs and topped by my mother's home-made raspberry jam.

Then I went out in the back garden. Not to look at the raspberry canes or to do a little light weeding. No, I spent the next two hours kicking a football against the pebble-dashed wall of the house. I'd been doing this on a regular basis for over four years and I could now bring the rebounds instantly under control. Mum knew that I was also controlled enough not to break the kitchen window. But she'd been worried for some time that I was going to damage the dashing. On that interminable Sunday evening, however, she said "nowt" and let me get on with it.

Monday morning dawned wet and chilly. April in Bradford was very different from April in Paris. I forced down some breakfast – home-made marmalade instead of jam. No bread and dripping in our house, thankyou very much. Dripping was kept for cooking those sublime fish and chips.

Machinery in the nearby mill had been thundering away for some time when, suitably gloved and duffel-coated, I climbed aboard the Lambretta feeling nervous as well as troubled. Would I finish up at "'t' mill" like most of the blokes round here?

I had to be at the manager's office by 10 am and I set off in good time. The journey to the Town's ground at Leeds Road normally took about 40 minutes. I'd take the Wakefield Road out of Bradford before cutting off through a little village called Low Moor to pick up the main road to Huddersfield. By now the early drizzle had settled into a steady downpour. The duffel-coat that Mum had bought me cut-price from the mill was sodden as I approached a hump-backed bridge. Rather too quickly, as it turned out.

The road was very greasy and the scooter skidded on the other side of the hump's summit. Off I came. But I was still clinging on to the handlebars in the hope of retaining my beloved Lambretta as I skidded along on the middle of the road.

Coming towards me was a double-decker bus. I can see those big wheels now. Yes, I'd had a depressing weekend but, no, I had no wish to fling myself under a bus. At that point, alas, I seemed to have no choice in the matter. Never mind the end of my dreams; it suddenly seemed as though the end of my life was fast approaching.

Thanks Shanks

CHAPTER SEVEN

Bill picks up the bill

The bus stopped dead. Which is more than I did. Still clinging to the handlebars of my scooter, I sailed past the stationary front wheel, missing it by inches, and finally came to a halt a few yards on. The driver leapt out of his cab and rushed over to ask "Are you all right, son?"

He would have helped me up but I was already on my feet, albeit somewhat shakily, embarrassed as well as bruised. Thankfully, the scooter was all right too. It started first time as I clambered back aboard, bade farewell to the bus driver and set off towards Huddersfield minus a duffel-coat button or two. I now felt dishevelled as well as depressed and anxious. But at least those gloves had ensured that I wouldn't have to shy away from shaking Shankly's hand on the basis that I was too muddy or too bloody. Or both.

The duffel-coat came off as soon as I stepped inside the main entrance to the Leeds Road ground and sat down in reception. I'd decided to keep it carefully folded over the left arm of my one and only suit. It had been bought from Dunn and Co who billed themselves as

"Hatters". They were also "Suiters", albeit with an 'e' rather than an 'o' after the 't'. This one was made of good Yorkshire worsted. I was hoping desperately that the collar and tie beneath it hadn't been sullied by impact with the wet Tarmac of Low Moor. There would probably have been a mirror in the gents, but I couldn't go and check in case I missed the call from on high.

It wasn't long coming. Somebody appeared to say "Mr Shankly will be with you shortly." And he was. Having a glove-stuffed crash helmet in one hand and my duffel coat over the opposite arm, I didn't feel able to shake hands. But he quickly put me at ease. "Come with me, David," he said. "You'll be all right," he added in a strange echo of my mother's favourite phrase.

I followed him down the corridor and into the office once occupied by Herbert Chapman, the manager who brought the Roaring '20s to Huddersfield. There would have been more silverware in the trophy cabinet in his day. As it was, cups and shields were somewhat thin on the shelves in there. Nor were there many framed photos around the wood-panelled walls. It all seemed a little austere. The chair that I was offered was hard and high-backed with no padding on the seat. Shankly told me to "pick it up and bring it round here". Having tentatively released coat and helmet, I duly did as I was bid, circumnavigating the large desk between us. There were no barriers with Bill. He leaned towards me as though letting me in on something said strictly in confidence. Can't remember the exact words now but it went something like this:

"I know that I've upset you, David. I also know that you'll have had a rotten weekend. But there's no other way of doing it." There was a bit of a pause before he added "It's almost been as bad for me because I don't like doing it. But it's a [expletive deleted] hard world out there. You won't believe this but I've made the best decision for you. You've got a certain talent but not enough to make you into a successful professional footballer. So I've got to do something about it now rather than in 12 months or two years time. It means that you can do something about it. You're not going to like me for what I've done but it's the right thing."

Then he said something that I'll never forget, "This club is my extended family. So you're one of my family and I'm going to look after you. What do you want to do?"

Obviously he knew that I needed to find work. But such was my level of self-pity at the time that I couldn't resist telling him "I've given up a good job. I've got no qualifications and I'm a failed footballer. I also failed at school, so I haven't got a lot to offer."

The benign and paternalistic Shankly disappeared for a moment. "Now you're making me cross," he growled. Then he glowered at me so fiercely that it was almost as if I was staring into floodlights. "You have a lot to offer," he went on. "And I'm going to help you, David. But I won't help you if you're not going to make an effort. So I'll ask you again: what do you want to do?"

"I don't know," I almost whispered, shifting around uncomfortably on that hard chair.

"Well, I'll tell you then. Look how you've looked after Denis. Now that takes some doing because he's different. Look at the number of times you got people out of trouble. Have you thought about that? As I said, you've got a lot to offer." Then he paused briefly before adding "I think you'd be a great teacher."

At that point you could have knocked me off the chair with a blackboard rubber. I gulped and stammered "Mr Shankly, I've got no GCEs because I was told at school that I wasn't very bright."

"That's nonsense," was the curt Shankly dismissal of

my former head teacher Mr Cook's assessment of my worth. This was a man, remember, who had grown up in severe poverty in a small Scottish mining village and had left school at 14 to work down the pit.

"What do you need to be a teacher?" he enquired in the almost bemused manner of a man venturing into alien territory.

"Qualifications."

"Go and get it sorted, and this is what I'm going to do," he said, bemusement replaced by a snappy decisiveness. "First of all I'm going to get you a job to earn some money. In the meantime, I want you to find out how much it would cost for you to go to college or night-school, or do whatever you've got to do. And then let me know because, as I said, I want to help you."

Bear in mind that I was a 16-year-old with no future as a pro' and he was the hugely ambitious manager of a club that had been the first to win three successive League titles. As it turned out, he would fulfil his ambitions elsewhere. And how! Yet this man, who liked to portray himself as a fully-focused football obsessive, took an interest in an apparent no-hoper in whom he saw something different. That says everything about him, his philosophy and the background that had forged it.

It certainly had a massive impact on me. I suddenly felt as though a great burden had been lifted. What he'd done was to resurrect my spirit and make me think, yes, I could make something of my life. If Bill Shankly thought I had something to offer then who was I to argue?

Our meeting had lasted about 15 minutes. As I stood up, I made sure that I had a free hand to shake with Shankly's. I may have been a big strong lad for my age but his grip was like a vice. "I want you to come back to me within a week," he said as we parted outside his office door.

I promised that I would while furtively manipulating my fingers under the weight of my still damp duffel coat, as if to check that no bones had been broken. For all that, the ride home seemed a lot less pained than the outward journey had been. No near-death experiences either. All I could think about, through Low Moor, the road into Bradford and the climb up Horton Bank Top was "Who am I going to ask about getting these qualifications?"

Not Mr Cook, that was for sure. As I disclosed in an earlier chapter, I wouldn't set foot in my former headmaster's office for another 40 years or so. Instead I went to see the teacher at Buttershaw who had taken far more interest in me than any other. Steve Allott would go on to become a Football League referee. But in those days he was responsible for the only three activities at which I excelled at school: football, cricket and PE.

"I need some help in getting a GCE in English," I mumbled. "And then four others," I added before going on to explain about my recent trip to Huddersfield.

To my surprise, he responded by saying "Bill Shankly's absolutely right. You could be a very good teacher. So leave it with me. I'll get you a tutor to help with your English." And he did. Not my original English teacher, as it turned out, but a Mr Cox. He was a kind man. Patient, too, which was just as well. Bear in mind that I hadn't taken an exam since failing the eleven-plus.

Mr Allott also told me about an organisation in London called the Rapid Results College that dealt in correspondence courses. They sent me the details and the cost. To me it seemed an astronomical amount to acquire the four O-levels that I would need, on top of English, to get into a teachers' training college. There would have to be at least two A-levels as well, but that was still some way down the line.

When I told Mr Shankly about the cost, he didn't flinch. Nor did he renege on his promise. The money was forthcoming in a bulging white wedge of an envelope - far more than I'd ever seen before. Neither I nor my parents had a bank account at that time, so a cheque would have been out of the question.

I had to earn some money of my own, of course, and Huddersfield Town's manager was as good as his word on that issue as well. For the next three years I would see rather a lot of shelves. I'd be stacking them at Marks and Spencer and then, after working through my lunch break, I'd be off to the nearby library at 4.30 on the dot. When it came to acquiring qualifications, I was on my way.

Unfortunately, Bill Shankly was on his way as well. Yes, he had a rising star in the firmament in Denis Law. But he knew that top managers, including Manchester United's Matt Busby, had been sniffing around. And he doubted that Huddersfield's directors had the will or the ambition to hold on to Law and build a great side around him. Liverpool were also in the second flight at the time. But when he was approached by their chairman, Tom Williams, he evidently sensed a far greater potential.

Denis would sign for Manchester City in March, 1960, for £55,000, a British record at the time. Many a Premier League player today wouldn't get out of bed for that much money every week, but no matter. Of far more concern to the young David Kershaw was that Shankly had headed across the Pennines even earlier than Law. He was on his way in early December, 1959, shortly after I'd failed O-level English for the first time. It wouldn't be the last. But had I seen the last of the manager who would – eventually – transform my life?

Not quite.

Nor had I seen the last of his money. Shankly was as good as his word. He may have been busy transforming Liverpool FC from Second Division also-rans into League Champions, but he still ensured that there would be an envelope stuffed with notes waiting for me at regular intervals in the little makeshift office next to the changing rooms at Cleckheaton. I would take it to the post office and transform it into a postal order to be despatched to Rapid Results.

Still to come was a memorable Merseyside Saturday when – at last – I would have some good news to tell him.

Thanks Shanks

CHAPTER EIGHT

An Eccles cake at Anfield

There was no wine on sale at the Bradford branch of Marks and Spencer in the late 1950s and early '60s. No fancy food either. There was fruit, mind you. It came all the way from Great Yarmouth in a lorry. And once a week it was my turn to be in the narrow street at the back of the store by 6.30 am to help the assistant manager Fred Shackleton to unload it.

A rum character was Fred. Over 6ft tall, shaven-headed, very bombastic, he evidently harboured ambitions. "I'm going to become a senior manager at M and S," he assured me on more than one occasion. He played rugby league at an amateur level and liked to throw his weight about. Even burly delivery drivers thought twice about arguing with him. He'd check the bananas that came in trays and pick odd ones out. Any skin slightly bruised or not the right shade of greenish yellow would be rejected. "I'm not having it," he'd snap and throw it back on the lorry. Having near-perfect bananas, apparently, was a way to prove your managerial metal.

I do remember one of the drivers protesting, only for Fred to thrust his ugly mug almost into his face before warning "You bugger me about and you'll lose the contract." When I once summoned up the courage to point out that he'd been a bit rude, he confided "Look, lad. I want the best for this shop because that's my future. They can save the rubbish for Manchester." Then he said something that has stayed with me to the extent that I repeated it regularly during my career as a head teacher. "You look after the little things," said Fred, "and the big things look after themselves."

Fruit was a only a little part of the retail offer at the Bradford branch of Marks – and that was your lot on the food front. No Greek salads. No tomato and mozzarella on focaccia bread. The spécialité de la maison, as we rarely said in Yorkshire, was underwear. Substantial underwear. There were voluminous bloomers with double gussets and corsets that were anything but sexy. Lingerie sounded sexy but lingerie, like wine, was French and affordable only to mill owners and posh folk from down south. Had there been any silky briefs or camisoles on sale here, they would have looked like bits of froth tossed about on a sea of winceyette.

Nighties were designed to keep women warm rather

than to set their husbands aflame with desire. Warmth was a priority in the north of England in the days when central heating was a distant dream for most families. Men wore vests. White vests and white pants of considerable length and volume. Coloured "briefs" were still a few years away.

Every item that I unloaded and laid out on the shelves was labelled with the name of St Michael. He seemed to be the patron saint of underwear – Marks and Spencer's underwear anyway. And that's what the vast majority of us wore in Bradford and elsewhere.

Michael Marks, a Polish refugee, had started his retail career not far away. In Kirkgate Market, Leeds, to be precise, where he'd set up a stall in 1884. Ten years later he'd gone into partnership with a former cashier called Thomas Spencer and ten years after that they'd opened their first store in one of those opulent arcades in Leeds. I'm not sure when they expanded into Bradford and, to be honest, I didn't much care while lugging boxes of weighty wool and winceyette from the warehouse to the shop floor. All I cared about was my watch, a much-treasured Christmas present from one of the "Aunties", laboriously ticking its way to half past four. That meant that I could finally shed my overall and head for the library on the other side of Darley Street.

Don't get me wrong. I was grateful to Bill Shankly for securing me the job at Marks, which meant that I could make a contribution to the housekeeping and put some two-stroke fuel into the Lambretta. But I was even more grateful for the money that he was shelling out to ensure that I wouldn't have to do monotonous work like this for the rest of my life.

The four additional subjects that I'd chosen to do at O-level were Geography, History, British Constitution and Religious Education. I'd begun to realise that I didn't have a bad memory, despite heading all those heavy leather footballs, and the Rapid Results exam service sent booklets packed with facts that were designed to be memorised if not always fully understood. That venerable library, with its seemingly endless shelves and glinting glass cases full of leather-bound tomes, was an imposing setting for an impressionable lad. And those formidable librarians, grey hair scraped back into bulbous buns for the most part, provided the peace and quiet in which those "facts" could be absorbed. They shushed the merest whisper into silence.

There were a lot of staff members about, only two of them men, who were bossed about mercilessly by those fearsome women. The women were middle-aged to elderly, for the most part, the men somewhat younger. Smartly dark-suited, they were expected to jump to and climb steep steps to replace or pluck books from the higher shelves.

The library was open late into the evening and I'd stay until around 8.30, sustained by the odd banana or pear that Fred Shackleton had granted me if there'd been a surfeit towards closing time at M and S. Sometimes I'd nip to the canteen before leaving to supplement that fruity sustenance for my studies with a piece of parkin. A slightly gingerish cake made from oatmeal and treacle, parkin was something of a Yorkshire speciality.

The trick was to try to nibble a bit of cake or banana before being spotted by the most eminent of the grey-bunned "shushers". She'd be over like a shot and glower over her glasses. "You're not eating in this library," she'd proclaim in a magisterial manner that sounded all the more threatening in the silence that prevailed elsewhere. On one occasion, when I was feeling particularly peckish, I tried another nibble after an hour or so – only to discover that the same woman seemed to have eyes in the back of her bun. She came striding over and snatched the parkin from me. "I've told you once," she thundered, "no eating." And off she went, brooking no argument. Turned out that she was the head librarian. I could see why. I could also see one of those cowed male librarians having a little snigger.

Ah, well. At least Mum would have something in the oven for me when I got home around nine. Yes, it was usually cold brisket, but there was some gravy to warm it up a bit. And there was always rice pudding to follow.

My battle with GCE English examiners, meanwhile, continued apace. The ever-patient Mr Cox would knock on our front door at regular intervals and be shown by my mother into the peace and quiet of the front parlour where I'd be waiting for him. Having failed in November, 1959, I sat the exam again in January 1960. Result: another failure. But at least I was getting used to the examination process. The Cox strategy seemed to be to enter me for as many exams as possible and cover all bases. Come the summer, I found myself sitting the same subject for three different examining boards: Joint Matriculation, London and Associated Examining.

It was the latter that finally provided me with a lowish grade success at what had been, effectively, the fifth attempt. A bit of a scrape-in, you might say. No matter. It was a pass. At last I would have some good news to tell

An Eccles cake at Anfield

Mr Shankly. The even better news for me was that he'd invited me over to see him and watch the first match of the new season. A ticket duly arrived in the post -- for a seat in the stands, no less. Long before kick-off time, however, I would be expected to meet the manager at the ground.

I was up at the crack of dawn, just as I used to be in the days of away matches at Roker Park, Sunderland. This time, though, there'd be no coach to convey me. No team-mates either, and no steak and chips on the way home. I was going to be on my own for a very long time. The journey from Horton Bank Top to Anfield by public transport involved two buses and two trains: Bradford to Leeds and then Leeds to Liverpool. Mum, bless her, had given me the fare, plus a bit extra, and some sandwiches wrapped in greaseproof paper.

When we finally pulled into Lime Street Station with its great, if grubby, glass and iron roof, it was like stepping into a different land where everybody spoke a different language. Scouse, needless to say, and it had yet to become nationally fashionable.

Beatlemania was two or three years away. Cilla Black was still Priscilla White and Gerry's Ferry 'Cross the Mersey had yet to set sail – in vinyl at least. As for Jimmy

Tarbuck, he wouldn't be reducing the nation to tears of laughter for a few years yet. Stand-up comedy is a tough business in any city and Tarby's journey around Liverpool's pub-and-club circuit must have involved plenty of competition.

Everybody in this strange city seemed to imagine that they were a comedian. The bus to Anfield proved an early introduction to this phenomenon. I was still marvelling at the imposing, if sooty, civic buildings around the station when I stepped aboard the back platform that was common to all buses in those days. The conductor's eyes lit up with mischief. "Bloody hell, you look posh," he said. Yes, I'd dug out the Dunn and Co suit from the mothballs. My best tie too, and Mum had meticulously ironed my white shirt. "Are you seeing anyone important?" the conductor enquired.

I nodded and mumbled something, but didn't mention Bill Shankly. Too embarrassingly boastful, I decided, before scuttling off to sit down on one of the many seats that were available so long before kick-off time. The conductor was right behind me, ticket machine at the ready, and a joke to follow. "What do you call a Liverpool fan in a suit?"

Short pause while I looked at him blankly.

An Eccles cake at Anfield

"The accused."

Laugh? I couldn't start. But I did manage a wan smile. "Hope you haven't been a naughty boy," he added, still chuckling to himself as he lurched back to the platform.

When I finally got to the ground and shook the Shankly hand again, I was braced for the bone-cruncher and ready to respond in kind. When I told him that I'd passed my first O-level, he responded as though I'd been awarded a double first from Oxford. His beaming grin could have lit up Anfield had it been a murky November night rather than a sunny day in late August. "Come on," he said, heading for the office door, "I'll buy you a pint to celebrate."

Although I was still a few months short of my 18th birthday, there was no doubt that I looked old enough to be served alcohol in a pub. But that wasn't the problem. The great manager's floodlit smile faded only a flicker when I felt obliged to tell him that I was a Methodist and didn't drink. My former team-mates would have laughed derisively. The vast majority of Liverpool fans would think that I was stark raving mad. Bill Shankly had just offered to buy me a pint and I'd declined.

We went to a cafe somewhere near the ground and

he bought me a cup of tea and an Eccles cake instead. At one point in our brief conversation, he leaned over, looked me straight in the eye and said "I know you're going to make it." And suddenly I felt about 9 ft tall. The man who would go on to be immortalised in Liverpool and become a legend to football fans way beyond the city's boundaries had given me back my self-confidence. All too soon we exchanged another bone-cruncher and he was off to the dressing room to spread more self-confidence among his first-team players.

I would never see him again. But the money to pay for my belated education would keep coming. As a result, Shankly's effect on my life would be incalculable.

His effect on Liverpool FC has been well recorded. Promotion to the First Division was still a season away. There would be more. Much more. For now it was the beginning of a season where they would finish third in Division Two, just missing out. Yet already there was a buzz about the place. I sensed that soon after showing my stand ticket to the man on the turnstile, another would-be comedian. "Good job you're not on the Kop," he confided with a knowing wink. "They've got their Echos rolled up on there."

I didn't have a clue what he was on about. Much later

An Eccles cake at Anfield

I realised that he was referring to the Liverpool Echo which, like many a local newspaper, came in handy for far more than transmitting news of road accidents and court cases. In the chip shop where my Mum had worked, pages from the Bradford Telegraph and Argus were wrapped around battered haddock and chopped spuds infused with beef fat. Here rolled-up versions of the Echo were used to conceal something far less appetising. They were a convenient urinary outlet at a time when it was so crowded on that terrace that getting to the Gents was a distant dream. Many a Koppite, I suspect, had savoured a pint or three before the match. Unlike yours truly, none of them would have turned down the offer of one from Bill Shankly. They would have been honoured, delighted, overwhelmed.

The Anfield atmosphere was already building when I took my seat, only two or three blocks from the directors' box. What a view! I'd never seen anything like it or, indeed, heard anything like it. The noise from the Kop was extraordinary by kick-off time. What must it be like to play in front of a crowd like that? I couldn't help asking the question and feeling a twinge of envy for those who, unlike me, had been able to follow their dreams and play professional football at a decent level.

Thanks Shanks

As a former centre-half, I could never have imagined in my wildest dreams scoring a volley from just outside the area and seeing so many happy people surging towards me. But that's what the Liverpool left-winger had just done. Couldn't remember his name until I recently looked it up on line. It must have been Kevin Lewis, scoring on his debut and considered good enough to keep Ian Callaghan out of the side. Not for long as it turned out. The other scorer was Dave Hickson, a former Everton player who'd briefly played for Huddersfield under Shankly. Small world. Playing alongside him up front was one Roger Hunt, or "Sir" Roger as he was dubbed by Liverpool fans. He would go on to play for England in the fabled final of the World Cup, 1966.

Final score: Liverpool 2 Leeds United 0. No wonder there were so many glum faces on the first part of my long train journey home. Not that it bothered me as a Bradford lad. All I could think about was Bill Shankly telling me that he knew that I was going to make it as a teacher.

I was more determined than ever to prove him right.

CHAPTER NINE

Cricket, unlovely cricket

At least I still turned out occasionally for a Bradford City side. Bradford City Council's first XI, alas, rather than Bradford City FC. My Dad was a council employee, of course, and occasionally he'd ask me to step in at the last minute if he'd heard that the team was a man short. Well, at least it made a change from the cramped confines of my bedroom, the counterpane strewn with booklets from Rapid Results. And that, in turn, made a change from the imposing expansiveness of the Central Library opposite Marks and Spencer, where I worked on weekdays only.

The standard of football in those matches of municipal rivalry was somewhat below what I'd become used to. I absolutely ran the show, lording it about the field like the Franz Beckenbauer of the Bradford side – if, that is, Beckenbauer had been around at the time. It would be a few years yet before the German maestro would impress himself on the English consciousness.

Infrequent forays back on to the football field aside, there were few breaks from studying or stacking shelves

95

– during the winter months at least. The Methodist church round the corner offered the only respite. Apart from attending services on Sundays, I'd sometimes pop in on Saturday mornings to the basement beneath the church for cup of tea or an orange juice with friend Philip. My goodness, we lived on the wild side.

Coffee?

Never touched the stuff. Admittedly coffee bars had started to appear in the middle of town. I could hear Elvis or Eddie Cochran, Buddy Holly or Ottilie Patterson, wailing or wafting, booming or blasting from the jukebox as I scurried past. Occasionally I'd stop and peer through the steamy windows. The coffee appeared to be some light-brown liquid topped by scummy froth and served in cups of see-through glass. And the clientele tended to be dominated by die-hard teddy boys or what passed for Bohemia in the Bradford of the early '60s.

While they lounged about, I had work to do. The only escape from the world I was heading towards, a permanent job at Marks and Spencer's, was to get some qualifications. Fred Shackleton's ambition was to become the manager there. Mine was to get out as soon as possible. I didn't like Fred, but I admired his capacity to be the first to arrive and the last to leave every day. If nothing else, he confirmed for me that hard graft was the way to get on. And Bill Shankly's assertion that he knew that I could do it had provided not only inspiration but a growing self-confidence.

What's more, I was beginning not just to absorb the contents of those booklets but to understand them. Studying was becoming more than facts, facts, facts to be absorbed, like a pupil of Dickens's tyrannical teacher Thomas Gradgrind. History was no longer just a sequence of events and dates any more than geography was about memorising maps. The importance of the 1832 Reform Act to the British constitution was becoming as evident as the significance of Islam to the Middle East and, indeed, parts of Bradford.

So pleased had my personal tutor Mr Cox been when I'd finally scraped a pass at O-level English that he was more than happy to arrange more exams in more subjects with more than one examining board. Result: four more GCEs in the summer of '61. Okay they were all at the lowest possible pass grades. But it still meant that I could write to Shankly and tell him that I had five O-levels, no less.

I received a letter back, evidently typed by his secretary, expressing his delight and confirming that he would carry on paying until I made it to teachers' training college.

There was just one problem. My chances of adding maths to my growing list of qualifications defied any formula known to man. Yet a pass in maths was required to train as a teacher. I was conscious of that. So was Mr Cox. And I could sense his anxiety that I was making no progress whatsoever. Together we went to see my other mentor, Steve Allott. He had moved from Buttershaw School to a teacher-training college in Saltley, Birmingham, but at weekends he came back to see his family in Bradford.

Once again Mr Allott did a lot for me. "I'm going to tell the principal," he said, "that we've got this ex-footballer who'd very keen and he's going to be a great teacher. But he's no good at maths. Could you find a way of letting him in?"

The short answer to that turned out to be "yes". The college was called St Peter's and the principal appeared keen to welcome a staunch Christian who just happened to be a useful footballer. I was in. Or rather I would be, Mr Allott informed me in his role as go-between, as long as I could acquire the two A-levels required.

Something else was required at that point: another

letter to Bill Shankly. Back came an immaculately-typed response, as steadfast as ever. Yes, he would carry on paying for as long as it took.

Time to get the head down again. More booklets arrived from Rapid Results. More British Constitution. More Religious Education. More difficult to understand than anything I'd tackled so far, apart from maths. More time in my bedroom then and, yes, even more time in the library. But on summer Saturday afternoons at least, I found some spare time to indulge my other great sporting love.

I played for Great Horton Cricket Club's second team in the Bradford League. Every suburb in the city had a cricket ground in those days. Few were what you might call scenic. Ours was bordered by a terrace of back-to-back houses. Rather different from the Cotswolds where my son Richard now plays for a team called the Ramblers. The pitch and outfield, mind you, were maintained to a very high standard. Even at second-team level, cricket was a serious business in Yorkshire and we were expected to play to win at all costs. A "gentleman's game" it was not. Sledging was par for the course long before Ian Chappell's Australian side of the '70s hit the headlines with their bruising comments about English batsmen.

Thanks Shanks

A thick skin was a pre-requisite for a Bradford batsman. As I strode out from the pavilion, still in my teens, mid-on and mid-off would shake their heads with foreboding. "You're in for trouble lad," one of them would predict. "He's after your foocking head," the other would add, nodding towards a well-built man, ball in hand, and just about visible in the middle-distance. He would be practically pawing the ground with his boot at the start of an extremely lengthy run-up. There were no helmets in those days and you could be assured that plenty of bouncers would be coming your way. Plenty of abuse, too, from those rumbustious bowlers who seemed to carry on after sending down a particularly vicious delivery. They'd be glowering at you from what seemed not much more than a few yards away.

As you took guard for the first ball, the slips would start. "This kid fancies himself," first-slip might observe. Second-slip would concur before adding "We'll soon put him right." Then you'd play and miss at the first ball. "Hah. Bit of a joker, isn't he?"

"Ay, he is. Wonder how long he'll stay."

Only once do I remember staying long enough to make a half-century against a team called Drighlington. The slips and wicket keeper had shut up by that time. Until, that is, I hit a couple of fours through the covers off one of very few spin bowlers.

"Foocking hell, that's good," exclaimed first slip.

"Ay, not bad"

Praise indeed.

Praise from the crowd was sparing, to put it mildly. First-team matches would attract attendances of 250 or so, and slightly over half that number would turn out to watch us seconds. For the most part they would sit, arms folded. A decent cover drive, square cut or shot off the legs and through mid-wicket might persuade them to unfold those arms and bestow some welcome applause. Occasionally one or two would bawl some advice that wasn't always easy to catch. Just as well, perhaps, as it tended to be blunt to the point of rudeness.

They would have a whip-round, mind you, for a century or even a fifty. My half-century was rewarded with just over a tenner. But some members of the team would evidently have felt insulted by such a meagre return for their efforts at the crease. One of them was the aptly nicknamed 'Grumpy' Dinsdale.

He was a painter and decorator by trade, a rough diamond but a classy batsmen and one of the openers. I used to go in at three or four and, on one occasion, he was on 43 when I joined him out in the middle. We took a couple of singles and then he hit a four to take him to 49. Perhaps because I was desperate not to be out for a duck, I called for a risky run off the first ball of the next over.

Half way down the pitch, I suddenly changed my mind and scampered back to the crease. My calls to Grumpy to "stop, stop!" fell on deaf ears. He was left stranded as the wicketkeeper gleefully whipped off his bails. At which point he went berserk. "You fooocking idiot," he bawled, throwing down his bat. "That cost me 50 quid." Then slowly — very slowly — he trudged back to the pavilion, pausing every now and then to turn round and glare at me.

Not surprisingly, I wanted to delay my own return to the pavilion for as long as possible. Somehow I managed to grind my way to 20 or so before receiving an unplayable delivery. On my slow walk back across the outfield, I came to the conclusion that God would want me to apologise to Grumpy.

He was still bent almost double under his peg in the dressing room as I tentatively approached. "Don't you talk to me," he rumbled menacingly. As I backed away, it was noticeable that many of the rest of the team were struggling to control their sniggers and giggles. Grumpy was a vital part of the batting line-up but hardly the most popular member of the Great Horton side.

On this occasion at least, I wasn't reprimanded by the formidable Edgar Robinson – or Alderman Edgar Robinson, to give him his full title. The Club President, to give him his other title, was still swanning around the ground, shaking hands with members of the crowd who rose and doffed their caps in deference. (Most cricket-lovers in our neck of the woods sported flat caps in winter as well as summer. Only on those rare days when the sun beamed down without a brisk and bracing breeze, might a cap be replaced by a knotted handkerchief.) Needless to say, they were all men. The only women present on match days were in the kitchen, buttering bread and boiling water before emerging briefly to present us with substantial teas.

The Alderman dressed as an Alderman should. It may have been a Saturday afternoon, but the redoubtable Robinson circumnavigated the outfield suitably suited and booted. His black shoes gleamed in glimpses of sunshine. His stiff white collar was fronted by what could well have been a regimental tie, which in turn was secured by an enormous tie-pin. And his waistcoat, needless to say, was crossed by the standard northern aldermanic watch chain.

The deference shown to him by so many spectators had nothing to do with his position on Bradford City Council. He was respected as one of Great Horton's classier former batsman. Still held the club record for the highest score of 173.

Before each home game he would make his presence felt in the dressing room. "I don't want to see any flashing outside the off stump," he would proclaim in his gruff and gritty way, with an undercurrent of menace. His son, David, kept his counsel at these moments. As our captain, however, he made his own presence felt on the field. An old boy of Bradford Grammar School, he was more thoughtful and refined than his father – and, indeed, most of his team-mates. It was no surprise to learn that he later became a doctor.

He evidently thought that I had enough budding talent to be a top-order batsman. And maybe I could have made it into the first team had I gone to Tuesday-night coaching sessions in the nets at Bradford Park Avenue's ground. But instead of gripping a bat, I was busy coming to grips with the demands of the A-level booklets that kept arriving through the post from Rapid Results. With a modicum of success, it must be said. Come the summer of '62, a few months before my 20th birthday, I scraped through both exams with the lowest pass-grade possible. It was enough. Enough for me to write to Bill Shankly and tell him that I'd finally made it into teacher-training college. And, by the way, I'd be happy to come over to Liverpool to see him again.

He wrote back, via his secretary, to acclaim my letter as great news. He'd told me I could do it and I'd done him proud. No invitation, mind you, was forthcoming for another visit to a posh stand at Anfield. Not surprisingly, the manager had a lot on his plate at the time. Liverpool FC had won promotion back in the First Division and Shankly had much work to do before he could take his place as one of football's immortals. He was on his way.

So was I. Not to immortality but to an educational institution that I could never have imagined in my wildest dreams just a few years previously.

Birmingham beckoned.

Thanks Shanks

CHAPTER TEN

Goodbye Mum, hello Brum

Denis Law was back in Manchester. United rather than City this time. He was on his way to being crowned "The King" of Old Trafford after a brief spell playing for Torino in Italy where the locals must have seemed even more incomprehensible to him than the residents of Huddersfield and Cleckheaton had to one who'd rarely ventured beyond the borders of Aberdeen.

I began to understand how he must have felt when we arrived in Birmingham in September, 1962. The local accent proved to be impenetrable to three lads from Bradford, used to a broad Yorkshire bluntness of tongue. One of my travelling companions was Johnny Woodford, a very useful right-handed batsman who would hear many a blunt tongue when he finally made it into the Yorkshire dressing room at a time when Messrs Close and Illingworth, Trueman and Boycott were still talking to one another. But that would be a few years hence. For now he was heading south with myself and Trevor Overend, another of Steve Allott's former Buttershaw School sporting talents, bound for St Peter's College.

First we had to find the college. More specifically, we had to find somebody whom we could understand to tell us the way. "Orll roight, our kid?" beamed the first man whom I tentatively approached to ask where we might catch a bus to Saltley. What followed was a sing-song language mangling that evidently baffled Johnny and Trevor as much as me – judging, that is, by their blank expressions and subsequent shrugs.

Eventually we found somebody who was vaguely comprehensible and whose gestures seemed to imply that we needed to be at the far end of Corporation Street, Joseph Chamberlain's "Parisian boulevard" that stretched away opposite the hugely imposing Queen's Hotel. The Queen's was still standing. Just about. It would be gone in two years time. So would the adjoining Victorian station which boasted a roof with the broadest span in the railway world.

Like everything else here, it made me feel slightly insignificant and out of my depth. Bradford was a sizeable city but this place seemed enormous. Noisy as well. Planners had devised a scheme to destroy much of the Victorian heritage that had withstood German bombs and replace it with a city more accommodating to the motor cars made here and in nearby Coventry.

Goodbye Mum, hello Brum

Pneumatic drills rent the air. Scaffolding stretched skyward, up the side of ornately decorative buildings. Pick-axes and mallets were being wielded with wanton abandon.

Occasionally the drilling would stop and the Brummie accents of the demolition men would be interspersed with lilting Irish voices. Wolf whistles would ring out at regular intervals as they leered down on glimpses of cleavage or blonde beehive hair-dos.

We Bradfordians were used to seeing "immigrants", mainly from Pakistan. Here there were Sikhs and Hindus as well as Muslims, West Indians as well as Indians. Men from the Caribbean tended to sport trilbies at raffish angles. The women wore bright dresses that added some welcome splashes of colour to the greyness that prevailed.

Rather more elegant clothing graced the windows of Rackham's, the department store that we passed on our lengthy trek down Corporation Street. Much posher than Brown and Muff's, the nearest equivalent in Bradford. So posh that, in those days, Rackham's closed on Saturday afternoons to keep the hoi-polloi at bay.

There was nothing posh about those aboard the bus that we finally located to take us to Saltley. The conductor had such a strong Brummie accent that none of us understood his reply when I asked if he'd tell us when we reached College Road. Mind you, he was as good as whatever word he'd given us and made a point of coming to point out to us that our stop was the next one. It was time to step off the platform and stride into the institution that was going to change our lives. Once we'd picked up our bags, needless to say.

Not that I was carrying too much. To quote a Cliff Richard song from a few years earlier, I was travelling light. My mother had seen to that. She had despatched in advance a great big container with most of my clothes and given me strict instructions to send home my washing every week. She'd pay. None of those new-fangled laundrettes for her precious son.

To say that she had been upset by my leaving home was putting it mildly. She was devastated. Couldn't understand why I'd want to leave Horton Bank Top, let alone Bradford. To go to another city, 127 miles down south? Ridiculous. Yes, she'd supported my lengthy efforts to acquire qualifications. After all, that nice Mr Shankly had paid so much money. But, deep down, I know she'd have been much happier if I'd taken that job at the printers when I'd left school at 14.

Goodbye Mum, hello Brum

Dad was different. He'd been a grammar school boy, after all. And although he'd never been quite so effusive as to say "I'm proud of you", that's the feeling I'd sensed from his mates behind the goal when I'd made a rare visit to Bradford Park Avenue for a mid-week match. They evidently liked the idea of a lad who'd got his head down and grafted. Now, at long last, I'd made it to teachers' training college.

St Peter's was an imposing Victorian survivor, the weathered red-brick buildings ranged around a comparative rarity in north-east Birmingham: an open field. And no, it wasn't a sports field. Those of us budding teachers of physical education would travel to nearby Stechford to play football or cricket. Eventually, that is. On this memorable first day we were shepherded into a hall, welcomed by the senior tutor and split up before being shown to our accommodation. I was in the East Block where we shared communal toilets and baths at the end of a long corridor. At least we all had a private room. It seemed expansive to me after my box-room in Bradford. There was space for a desk as well as a bed. A bookshelf too. Not that I had any books. Here I was training to be a teacher yet, at that stage of my life, I had never read a novel.

Thanks Shanks

"I see that you're one of Mr Allott's protégés," said my personal tutor Mr Hughes on our introductory meeting. "Coming from Yorkshire, did you enjoy reading the Brontes?"

What could I say to that? Wuthering Heights might well have been Heathcliff Bank Top, if I'd known who Heathcliff or, indeed, Emily Bronte was. As for Jane Eyre, she might have been a girl at the Methodist youth club.

After due reflection, my response to Mr Hughes's original question was "Er . . . no." We didn't pursue that line of conversation any further. Instead he glanced at my notes again before remarking in his fruity drawl "I see that you have a major interest in football and are going to do PE. Oh yes and RE. What's your interest in religion? Do you believe in God?"

This time I was on firmer ground. "I can see the value of having a Christian faith," I responded. "That's one of the reasons why I'm pleased to be coming to a Church of England college."

"So you're an Anglican, are you?"

"No, I'm a Methodist."

"Oh, you're one of those non-conformists."

"Yes. And I'm rather proud of it."

Goodbye Mum, hello Brum

By then I was getting a teeny-weeny bit of confidence. Looking back, I can see that Mr Hughes was good at his job, putting me at ease and trying to tease out some answers to challenging questions.

The college was incredibly paternalistic with very strict rules. Visitors were expected to be out of our rooms by 10 pm. Particularly women. Mr Hughes used to come round shortly after 10 and knock on each door. Far louder and more threatening was a pounding on the woodwork from the deputy principal Mr Seeman, an Oxford graduate and a strict disciplinarian. One of my football team-mates was caught with a girlfriend in his bed and promptly sent down. To quote from Philip Larkin once more, "Sexual intercourse began in nineteen sixty three (which was rather late for me) – between the end of the Chatterley ban and the Beatles first LP." Well, at St Peter's it wasn't expected to begin at all.

At least we had a monthly visit from the young ladies of the Anstey College of Physical Education in Erdington – or Sutton Coldfield as they preferred to call it. Not that any of them spoke to me. Those Saturday night dances-cum-discos positively crackled with sexual energy. Most of my mates would be out on the floor eventually, twisting, jigging about or better still, smooching to the slow numbers. But I never once plucked up the courage to ask a girl for a dance. I remained shy and tongue-tied. Deeply frustrated too. And, yes, my fellow PE students took the Mick unmercifully. There was much discussion of matters sexual, but at least it wasn't anywhere near as crude as it had been in the changing room at Cleckheaton.

Perhaps because we expended so much energy on the playing fields and in the gym, none of us seemed to put on any weight despite the abundance of food on offer at St Peter's. All free as part of the deal. You could have a full English breakfast every day, whatever you wanted for lunch and then a three-course sit-down dinner every evening. There was even a top table worthy of a Cambridge college. No wine, mind you. And no passing the port. Still, our tutors sat in line on the stage, shrouded in gowns and capped by mortarboards. One exception was Mr Allott, who hadn't been to university. He had, though, shed his habitual tracksuit for a jacket, trousers and tie.

The principal, otherwise known as the Reverend Canon Pattern, sported a dog collar under his gown. We would all be expected to stand up as he resonantly said grace before every meal. And, yes, I was truly thankful for what I was about to receive, even if the food was a little on the stodgy side – in retrospect, that is. The main courses were meat and two veg, but at least the meat wasn't always brisket. As for the rice pudding, it wasn't anywhere near as good as my Mum's and the pastry around the apple pie took a bit of sawing through. No matter. It was the sort of food we were used to in the early '60s and the PE students among us had usually worked up a good appetite in the course of our "studies".

As for the RE, we were being prepared to teach rather than preach. We spent a lot of time discussing the sort of questions that adolescents might ask. What happens when you die? Is there life after death? Why does a loving God allow some people to suffer terribly when they don't deserve to? Why does the Bible seem to contradict itself in parts?

With the gentle encouragement of the lecturer, the Reverend Murray, I began growing in confidence and getting involved in these debates. In fact, I was really enjoying being at college. Didn't even feel a twinge of homesickness. But there was just one familiarly impenetrable cloud on the horizon.

We all had to do a basic course in maths in our first term, understandably enough. Half of the students were going to be teaching in primary schools. Luckily, I was bound for the secondary sector, but I was still expected to do two hours a week. And at the end of that first term we were all expected to pass a test or risk expulsion. I was terrified at the prospect of my inevitable failure. Being sent home to Bradford would be a humiliation. I would have felt as though I'd let everybody down, especially Bill Shankly.

The weekly two-hour maths session covered sums, fractions, percentages and other basic stuff. To me, however, it remained mumbo-jumbo. I had as much chance of getting the 40 per cent required for a pass as I had of being offered a record transfer fee to sign for Torino or Manchester United.

There was only one thing for it. After six weeks, I went to the maths tutor, Dr Norris, and told him how much I loved the college and wanted to stay there. What was I going to do?

"I'll have a word in someone's ear," he assured me. But I'd still be expected to complete the course and attempt the test.

The sum of my correct answers amounted to nought per cent. Even I knew what that meant. Mercifully, however, it didn't mean expulsion in my case. "This is a world record, David," Dr Norris confided in serious tones. Then his face crinkled into a broad grin before he added "It's a good job this is a godly college because I'm going to put you through."

Hallelujah! I felt genuinely happy at just being allowed to stay. What I didn't know at the time was that life in Birmingham was about to get even better.

Thanks Shanks

CHAPTER ELEVEN

Love's Young Dream in Summer Lane

It was time to head south again. Not *that* far south, to be honest, although it did take rather a long time to travel to Selly Oak on the other side of Birmingham. The journey involved two buses and a lengthy walk across the city centre. Was it worth it?

Oh, yes. And not just because it showed me a different side of the city from work-a-day Saltley where St Peter's was something of an architectural anachronism, surrounded as it was by factories, engine sheds and a prominent gas works. The second bus that I caught on that memorable Sunday afternoon passed down the tree-lined Bristol Road through Edgbaston, the city's most sought-after suburb. There were elegant houses bordered by large gardens and the expansive playing fields of King Edward's School, among other green spaces. At one point the clock tower of Birmingham University came into view. Little did I know at the time that I was about to feast my eyes for the first time on one of the university's undergraduates who would become the love of my life.

Why, you may ask, was I making this lengthy trip across town on a day when the bus timetable offered a restricted service?

There was Methodism in my madness. When I'd left Bradford, the minister at our local church seemed worried that I wasn't going to cope with Birmingham. Perhaps he could see that I'd lived a comparatively sheltered life. Whatever the reason, he had written to the Methodist Society in Selly Oak and they had duly invited me to one of their meetings. One of many as it turned out. This journey would become a regular part of my life – partly because I enjoyed listening to those Sunday afternoon debates over a cup of tea, but mainly because it allowed me to stay in touch with the young woman that I'd spotted on that very first visit.

There was something different about her. She stood out, even among the bright young things who seemed to know much more than me about world issues. Most of those present had come from grammar schools or had been educated in the independent sector. Although my confidence had been growing during my time at St Peter's, in this context I was acutely conscious of my Yorkshire accent. Old insecurities resurfaced ("you're a nice lad, David, but you're not very bright") and I kept quiet. So did the young woman. For a while at least. She'd listen to the debate unfold before intervening with a very practical and down-to-earth comment. And she'd make those telling interjections in a quiet, measured, almost down-beat way. I found her very attractive.

Needless to say, it took me weeks to get around to sitting next to her. Even longer to start talking. In the meantime, I'd acquired a more practical way of travelling across town. I'd been back to Bradford to pick up my scooter. And to see my parents, of course. Mum had seemed surprised that I was still in one piece, appeared well fed and full of life. In her heart of hearts, I think she would have loved me to have said that I hated Birmingham and wanted to come home. Instead I told her that I loved college and was looking forward to going back on Sunday afternoon. She was all too evidently disappointed. What's more, she was horrified that I was planning to go all that way on two wheels.

In the meantime, I'd been to Bradford Park Avenue with Dad and received a warm welcome from his mates. An even warmer one was forthcoming from the "aunties" at the Saturday-night card session. They made a tremendous fuss of me. So did my mother when I finally clambered aboard the Lambretta. There were tears in her eyes as she assured me that the washing that I'd brought back with me on the train would be sent on by post. As usual, she would bleach not just my football shorts and socks but also the laces of my boots. Greater love hath'd no Mum.

Plans to extend the M1 north towards Leeds were still three years away so the journey back, via Wakefield and Burton-on-Trent, had been lengthy and chilling. By the time I'd reached Sutton Coldfield I was beginning to wonder if my hands had been nibbled by frost-bite. But I'd made it back to Saltley with a full set of fingers. As for making it to Selly Oak the following Sunday, there would be no more endless waits at bus stops. No more dilly-dallying either.

I sidled into the seat next to the girl of my dreams and, during a break in the debate, plucked up the courage to say something to her. Immediately she put me at ease. Her name was Vivien but I could call her Viv. Her voice had a slightly Welsh lilt. She came from Hereford, apparently, but both her parents were from further west, over Offa's Dyke. Her Dad was the deputy treasurer of Herefordshire County Council who later became finance director of the Welsh Water Authority. There's posh, as they say in Wales. Much posher than my background, that was for sure.

Both parents were staunch Methodists and both expected big things of their extremely intelligent daughter. They expected her to train to be a doctor or a lawyer. Instead, with a characteristic show of independence, she'd told them that she wanted to be a social worker. Now she was one of the first students at the red-brick university up the road doing what was then called a Bachelor of Social Science degree. Part of the course involved living in at the Settlement, a care centre for elderly people in Summer Lane, Aston. Sounds lovely, Summer Lane. Believe me, it wasn't. Tradition had it that policemen had to walk around in pairs in that part of the inner-city. Prostitution was rife. Drug-dealing was getting underway, even in the early '60s.

Coming to Brum had been an eye-opener for Viv, even more so than it had been for me. It was the first time she'd seen back-to-back houses and people of colour. Yet she'd readily accepted leaving the sanctuary of the university campus to live on one of the city's roughest streets. For a while at least. And although she was only 18 and had just passed her driving test, she would take Settlement residents on day trips to Shropshire in a mini-bus. Some of those old Brummies were rum characters. I could only imagine what tales they told amid the raucous laughter on those lengthy forays into rural England.

Sometime Viv and I would stay behind together after Sunday afternoon debates at the Methodist Society and do the washing-up. It was on one of those occasions that I finally suggested with a matter-of-fact casualness that I certainly didn't feel, "I'll take you back to Summer Lane on the back of my scooter if you like."

She readily accepted. Encouraged and elated by her close proximity, I eventually pulled up outside the Settlement and decided that it was now or never. "Would you like to go out for a Chinese next Saturday," I mumbled. Then I took off my crash helmet and repeated the invitation. This time she heard me. And smiled. "That would be lovely," she assured me. "If you come round at 6.30, I'll be ready."

Elation knew no bounds at that moment. I sailed back to Saltley on a scooter that had somehow evolved into cloud nine. Couldn't wait for our date. And when Saturday finally came around, I must have summoned up enough charm over the chow mein to persuade Viv to come for another Chinese the following weekend. With a trip to the pictures for afters.

Love's Young Dream in Summer Lane

The film may have been Lawrence of Arabia or To Kill a Mocking Bird. Somehow I doubt that we went to see Lolita. To be honest, I can't for the life of me remember what we went to see. Not because I was slowly and surreptitiously trying get my arm around Viv's shoulder as darkness descended on the Gaumont. Oh no, it was far more embarrassing than that.

I fell asleep soon after the film started and woke up with a jolt just as the credits came up. My only excuse was that I'd been involved in a very hard and strenuous game of football that afternoon. Many a girl would have flounced off in a huff, irrespective of the apologies that tumbled out once we were back on the street. But Viv just shrugged it off with a humorous comment.

This was somebody very special, I realised, as our relationship blossomed. By the end of the summer term, my first year at college and hers at university, I was about to put her good-humoured tolerance to the ultimate test. She would come with me on the back of the Lambretta to meet my Mum and Dad. Not to mention "Uncle" Eric and the "aunties".

Talk about a culture shock. For a young lady from a respectable middle-class family, settling in the Summer Lane Settlement was a doddle compared to staying at

Horton Bank Top, Bradford. Uncle Eric duly arrived, opened his voluble mouth and promptly inserted his size 12s. "Do you know you're going to have the mother-in-law from hell?" he boomed at Viv.

Talk about embarrassing. We hadn't even discussed getting married at that stage. The silence that followed was like one of those prolonged pauses in a Harold Pinter play. Any minute now, I thought, Eric will start banging on about "Pakis". It was a great relief when he finally set off with Dad on their long trek for a Friday-night pint. With icy propriety, the potential mother-in-law-from-hell showed Viv to my sister's former bedroom, Ann having left home at the earliest opportunity. Needless to say, I would be sleeping in the box-room with my parents' room between us. No hanky-panky, thank-ye. Of course not. Neither of us would have considered sneaking about in the dead of night like characters in a French farce. There was a rather sweet innocence about our relationship.

We were simply sitting on the settee the following evening while watching television – a comparatively recent addition to the front parlour. The aunties had come and gone. Card games were over for another week. Even Mum and Dad had gone to bed. Or so I thought. Ten minutes or so after they'd gone upstairs, Mum came down again, peered in the parlour and proclaimed "You two are holding hands." (By now we seemed to have moved from a Pinter play to a scene from one of those grainy cinematic adaptations of a so-called "kitchen-sink" novel.) "Come on. Off you go to bed."

As usual, I didn't argue. Just did what I was told. So did Viv. When we talked about it the following day, she seemed to accept that that was the way it was "oop north". Such was her remarkable tolerance that she came back to Bradford with me on other occasions. One stands out in my memory and causes me embarrassment to this day.

We were in the kitchen-diner (not holding hands) when my mother announced "David, the Tiller Girls are on at the City Varieties in Leeds. I've got two tickets so that you can go with one of your mates. Viv can stay here and we'll have a good chat." Then she added with her usual sensitivity, "It'll be a chance for you to see some really good legs." Viv could have been deeply offended and rightly so. But Viv, being Viv, said nothing. As for me, I just went along with Mum's wishes as usual. All I could think about as the Tiller Girls kicked and clicked their high heels around that old music-hall stage was my girlfriend

Thanks Shanks

feeling obliged to make sandwiches with my mother
while the aunties gossiped and giggled over hands of gin
rummy in the smoke-filled fug of our parlour.

CHAPTER TWELVE

The Joys of Hereford and Handsworth

It's a wonder that Viv ever agreed to go back to my parents' house again. But she did. This was a student, remember, who came from a comparatively privileged background yet was prepared to spend part of her time at university living and working on one of the roughest streets in Birmingham. Summer Lane, Aston, and Ledbury Road, Hereford, belonged to different planets. Yet "scootering" from one to the other was a doddle compared with the one from Brum to Bradford, as I was about to discover.

My first contact with anyone from her family had been when Viv had gone home for some reason and I'd rung the house after a prolonged search for a red telephone box containing a phone that actually worked. The number that I dialled has stayed with me to this day. So has the voice of the woman who picked up the receiver. It seemed so sophisticated and articulate. Her mother was all too evidently different from mine.

"Is Viv there?" I enquired hesitantly, conscious once more of my Yorkshire accent.

"Oh, hello, is that David?"

"Yes."

"Oh, David, we've heard so much about you and we're so looking forward to meeting you."

She then passed me on to Viv who made arrangements for that meeting. We were going to go to Hereford in a few weekends time. Together. On the Lambretta. And as we scooted through increasingly stunning countryside, my nervousness was increasing with each passing mile. What would her posh parents make of a lad from a council estate in Bradford?

In other respects, my confidence had risen markedly during my time at St Peter's. I was enjoying training to be a teacher and just knew that it was the right profession for me. How Bill Shankly had seen that will always remain a mystery. I had been reading more and more. Not novels; not yet. But I was becoming engrossed in books about politics and theology, sociology and psychology. I'd become fascinated by the Swiss psychologist Jean Piaget and his theories about cognitive development. Meanwhile, Donald Soper had become something of a hero. He was not just a Methodist non-conformist but also a socialist and a pacifist – a stance that didn't make him too popular in the wake of the Second World War. As a child, I'd been with my Dad to see him talk on the steps of Bradford Town Hall and some members of the crowd had thrown tomatoes at him. Now I was reading books by him as part of my RE course.

The PE course was even more enjoyable – apart, that is, from a brief but compulsory dalliance with rugby. I'd already become a lynchpin of the college football team, along with one Howard Riley who'd played for Leicester City and could kick a dead ball harder than anyone I'd ever seen. There was a strong competitive element among would-be PE teachers and I took a fair few knocks at centre-half, particularly in matches against our arch-rivals from St Luke's College, Exeter. Bruising encounters on the field didn't bother me. So it wasn't the roughness of "rugger" that put me off; there just seemed to be too many hold-ups and petty rules. And the whole process of passing and receiving that oval ball never came as naturally to me as trapping a round football or catching a cricket ball.

We were all expected to sample rugby, however, in case we were offered jobs in grammar or independent schools. Some chance! In my third year, our head of department, an ex-army man who dubbed himself Major

Osborne, set me up with an interview at the King's School in Worcester and I refused to go. It wasn't just that they played rugby rather than football. I had strong objections to working in a school where parents paid fees to send their sons.

By then I was becoming more politically aware. I'd taken to reading The Guardian, which had recently dropped the "Manchester" bit from its title. I also devoured The Observer every Sunday, even if its sports pages were dominated by rugby reports in those days. At least they found some room for an assessment of the 1963 Cup Final in which one Denis Law had scored the first goal for Manchester United in their 3-1 defeat of Leicester. By then he was already playing alongside another all-time great, Bobby Charlton. Still to come was the Old Trafford triumvirate of Law, Charlton and Best.

At the other end of the East Lancs Road, meanwhile, Shankly was working wonders at Anfield. Liverpool would win the first of three League Championships under his reign towards the end of my second year at college. Not to mention the FA Cup in my third year, beating Don Revie's Leeds United 2-1 in extra time amid some of the wildest celebrations seen at Wembley so far.

Strangely, I never mentioned to my fellow students

the part that Shankly had played in my life. Maybe that was partly because I didn't want it broadcast that I'd needed so much help to get where I was. Part of me, after all, was trying to put the past behind me. So I talked about the Liverpool manager as a leader, a character and a personality as one who had only read about him or seen him on the telly.

Not that we saw much TV at college. Apart the sports pages of The Guardian and the Observer, our main source of football news was Sports Report, which was then broadcast on the old BBC Light Programme. Somebody would have it on one of those new-fangled transistors in the dressing room after our matches. Eamon Andrews was the presenter and John Webster enunciated the results slowly enough for those checking their pools coupons to keep up. Waiting for the Bradford Park Avenue score seemed to take an eternity as, by that time, they were clinging on in Division Four. In the meantime, I'd listen out for the Liverpool and Huddersfield results. Manchester United, too. Denis, needless to say, featured prominently in post-match reports.

I never did see him from the terraces. Most Saturdays I was playing football myself, at a much lower level of course. On a rare weekend off I took Viv to Villa Park.

Thanks Shanks

Can't remember who Villa were playing now, but it certainly wasn't United. Or Liverpool for that matter. We were standing opposite the Holte End, a huge bank of terracing that seemed much steeper than the Kop. It wasn't so voluble, mind you, and not so packed with swaying and bouncing fans. Not on this occasion, anyway. Hopefully there was no need for any rolled-up copies of the Birmingham Mail or Evening Despatch.

One Villa player immediately caught my eye. Phil Woosnam was head and shoulders above the others. He was a cultured inside-forward, as we still called them in those days, and it came as no surprise to learn that he was a Welsh international. What was a surprise was to learn later that he'd studied physics at Bangor University and taught the subject at Leyton High School for Boys in the East End of London before signing for his first club, West Ham, in 1958.

Viv wasn't impressed by Woosnam or anybody else. She kept telling me that she was freezing. Admittedly, it was a very cold November day and you must feel it more if you're not remotely interested in what's going on out there on the field. It was the first and last time that I took her to a football match. She was altogether hardier on the back of the Lambretta, particularly as we headed west from Birmingham en route to Hereford.

Her parents' house on that main road towards Ledbury had been built sometime between the wars. It was semi-detached but big. Very big and very impressive. The front door was broad, high and inlaid with a stained-glass window. I'd never seen anything like it. Nor had I seen furniture of such evident quality. A peep into the front room confirmed that. The "lounge", as it was referred to, seemed to be at least twice the size of our parlour back in Bradford. And as for the kitchen at the far end of a wide and lengthy hall, it made the place where my Mum produced such fabled fish and chips and rice pudding seem like the cramped and poky little scullery that it was. Instead of an open range – essentially a little hearth with a small oven at the side – there was an Aga. The warmth it spread through this enormous kitchen was very welcome on a chilly November afternoon.

Beyond the window was an extensive back garden with outbuildings just about visible in the middle distance. Viv and I went out of the kitchen door to greet her father as he came in through the side gate after parking his gleaming Vauxhall Victor on the steep front drive. It was about an hour after we'd arrived and revelled in the warmth, not only of the Aga but also the tea served by Viv's mother, Doris, in bone china cups. I stifled an inclination to cock my little finger while sipping it.

Herbert Penhale looked as austere as you might expect from a senior accountant of his time. He was upright in stance and immaculately turned out in a three-piece suit. The handshake was firm and warm. Despite the austerity of his exterior, Herbert made conversation very easy. He was a big noise in the local Rotary Club, as well as the Methodist Church, and good at putting visitors at their ease. In retrospect, I can see that my own Methodism was a useful connection for him and Doris.

It was a tradition in their household to have a big, formal meal served in the dining-room at lunchtime every weekend. When the weighty cutlery was finally laid to rest, there was a lengthy discussion about world affairs before anybody thought about getting up again.

I was quiet at first, measuring things up. It soon emerged that, although Doris came from a socialist family in Wales, she was an avid Daily Mail reader. A Tory then. Herbert, on the other hand, was a classic Liberal of the old school, thoughtful and moderate. I began to chip in on our second visit. When Doris said something that I found difficult to accept, I would put an alternative point of view. Herbert liked that and encouraged me. I tried not to go in too hard for fear of upsetting my girlfriend's mother. To keep in her good books, I used to stand up and volunteer to wash up. Eventually, that is. Those debates were lively and enjoyable. It soon dawned on me that I'd been made far more welcome by the Penhales of Hereford than Viv had been by the Kershaws of Bradford. By Mrs Kershaw in particular.

Yet it was in Bradford rather than in Hereford, or Birmingham, where I finally popped the question. We were in my sister's former bedroom, to be precise. My parents were downstairs welcoming the guests for yet another Saturday-night card school. Very brave of us in the circumstances. Not that there was any impropriety, I hasten to add. I was sitting on the bed, both feet on the ground, while Viv was perched on a chair not much more than a foot away. Ann's old room may have been bigger than mine but it was still fairly cramped.

It was the beginning of our third year. I was 21 and she was 20. We both knew that we had to find jobs and I'd already decided that I wasn't going to move back to Bradford. Viv was the most important person in my life by then and I knew that it was about the last place on earth she'd want to live long-term. My mother would have made her life a misery.

We were feet apart in that bedroom and suddenly I just asked her in a matter-of-fact sort of way, "Would you be interested in marrying me?" Not the most romantic turn of phrase perhaps. The first five words might have been used by one of those door-to-door salesmen that were common at the time – "Would you be interested in buying a set of encyclopaedias?" And, no, I didn't get down on one knee.

Deep inside, however, I knew that this was the woman with whom I wanted to spend the rest of my life. Somehow it felt like the right time.

"Are you sure?" Viv enquired after a short pause.

"Absolutely sure."

This time there was no pause. "Yes," she beamed, "I will."

It took a while to come down, literally as well as metaphorically. When we finally went downstairs, Mum and Dad just happened to be alone in the kitchen, clearing away sandwich crumbs and putting plates in the washing-up bowl. There was nothing for it. We knew that we had to tell them there and then.

Dad, bless him, looked as pleased as he ever could and mumbled something appropriate, albeit with an anxious sideways glance at his other half. She had already "put on a face", as he would have put it. "Mmmm," she said. "This is a bit quick. You're very young."

She knew that we were both staunch Methodists and would never have been up to the sort of shenanigans that were usually the cause of early marriages in those days. All the same, her mood of seething unhappiness was maintained for the rest of the weekend. Rarely had conversation been so strained over the brisket and rice pud. Dad did his best by trying to talk about anything other than the prospect of a wedding in the not too distant future. Mum kept looking as though she was going to say something before sealing her lips into a downward curve. Viv just said, as diplomatically as possible, "Your Mum's finding this difficult." Something of an understatement in the circumstances. It was a great relief to climb aboard the Lambretta and head south again.

Being a third-year meant that I'd been allowed to live outside the confines of St Peter's halls of residence. I'd moved across Birmingham from Saltley to take a room above Handsworth Theological College. By then I was a preacher as well as a would-be teacher. Well, I did a bit of lay-preaching anyway, which was part of the Methodist tradition.

Handsworth was very much a place in transition at the time. Once the home of Matthew Boulton, James Watt and other key figures in the Industrial Revolution, many of its larger houses had now become packed with people from the Caribbean and the Indian sub-continent. Former citizens of the British Empire and Commonwealth were seeking to improve their lives by taking up the opportunities offered by bustling factories in the "Mother Country". Not to mention filling widely advertised vacancies for staff in the NHS.

There was a vibrancy about Handsworth. I could see it among the extrovert West Indian men outside pubs that I never ventured into and I could hear it in the hymns sung gustily and lustily, particularly by West Indian women, in church on Sundays. No screaming and clapping, mind you. Not in a Methodist place of worship, thank you very much. We'd leave that kind of thing to the evangelical churches that would soon be coming to joyful life in Handsworth and elsewhere.

Much as I liked the multi-cultural nature of the place,

I also became aware of the open and voluble racism that was rife at that time. There was much resentment among the old white working class, particularly those in the terraced streets off the main Soho Road, at the perceived threat that the "immigrants" posed to jobs and the prospect of better housing.

As I lay awake in my sparse room over the Theological College, profound questions kept going round and round in my head. How should the church react to strife on the streets? Why did a loving God allow so much hatred to fester both here and in the world beyond? How could Christianity co-exist with Hinduism, Sikhism and Islam? And how could I bring that message of co-existence into my future lessons as a teacher of religious education?

But one question above all others kept resurfacing on those occasional sleepless nights:

How on earth was my mother going to behave at our forthcoming nuptials when the Kershaws of Bradford would finally come face to face with the Penhales of Hereford?

Thanks Shanks

CHAPTER THIRTEEN

Wedded Bliss with a Cat that Hissed

As it turned out, I needn't have worried. Dad had "had a word". He'd discreetly assured me of that after we'd scootered back to Bradford towards the end of our student days. "The word" had evidently been delivered on one of those rare occasions when he'd asserted himself. I'd seen it once or twice before, usually when my mother had been particularly unreasonable towards my sister. "Come on," he'd snap. "This is ridiculous I'm not having you treating Ann like this." When it came to the forthcoming wedding, he had apparently told her, "Look, Alice, this is David and Viv's occasion. We don't want any unpleasantness or misunderstandings. Just behave yourself."

On reflection, I suspect that she'd enjoyed getting dressed up – a rare binning of the pinnie and an even rarer train journey. With friends. At least two of the "aunties" had travelled south and west, via Leeds and Birmingham. (My sister had come even further. Ann, bless her, had flown in from her new home in Geneva.)

Despite all those reassurances, I couldn't help taking

the occasional nervy glance in Mum's direction while sitting in the front pew in Owen Street Methodist Church, Hereford, toying with the ring in my suit pocket and waiting for the organ to strike up "Here Comes the Bride". I'd never seen her look so serene. Mum, that is. Viv simply looked radiant as she arrived on her father's arm and everybody's eyes were on her. Mine in particular.

The Bradford contingent had stayed overnight in Hereford, in a half-timbered pub called the Green Man. Now here they were in their best bibs and tuckers, occupying the pews on one side of the church. Apart, that is, from The Reverend Brian Rippin, long-time minister at my local church, who was now taking a leading role in today's service, and my best man Tony Lightowler. Tony had been a fellow student at St Peter's, having previously been another Bradford grammar-school boy, like my oldest friend Philip Lodge, who was now teaching in Nigeria.

On the other side of the aisle, the pews were packed with Penhales and their many friends. They included accountants, councillors and Rotarians. It was a big church and Herbert Penhale was a big wheel in a small city.

Wedded Bliss with a Cat that Hissed

My request for his daughter's hand in marriage had come after one of those leisurely meals in that imposing dining room on Ledbury Road. He just smiled and said nothing for a while. It was his wife who felt obliged to point out that Viv would be only 21 when we wed. "Isn't that a bit young?" she frowned, sounding a bit like my own mother for a fleeting moment.

"I'm sure, Doris, that they've worked that out," Herbert interjected, still smiling. Further discussion was brought to an end. No politics on that postprandial occasion. Debates were put on hold while Viv's parents promptly began planning the Big Day.

Both had easy social skills and they quickly put my own parents at ease when we moved on to the reception at the Three Counties Hotel. Mum seemed remarkably relaxed and happy. She was even prepared to let go – eventually – after giving me a big hug. Dad seemed to be enjoying himself, too, whether chatting to one and all over a pint or raising a glass of Asti Spumante for the toasts. My new father-in-law's speech was as polished as you might have expected from a prominent Rotarian. Tony did well, too, making the usual derogatory best-man jokes about the groom – about his awkwardness with women in my case. Viv smiled serenely.

Thanks Shanks

At one time I would have been terrified to have to make a speech to so many people. But now I was a fully-trained teacher. Standing in front of a captive audience and projecting my voice was going to be a large part of my professional life for the foreseeable future.

It was early August and the start of term was nearly a month away. No matter. I had a job lined up at the Arthur Mellows Village College, just outside Peterborough. Those village colleges combined education for local children with libraries for the wider community and seemed to be a speciality of the Fenlands. They'd been the idea of one Henry Morris, chief education officer for Cambridgeshire in the pre-war years. I'd done a dissertation on community education as part of my final qualifications from St Peter's. What's more, I'd received a distinction.

Yes, me – "not very bright David". I had a lot of people to thank for my transformation, not least my college tutors. Now I was really looking forward to being a teacher. Couldn't think of any job that would have been better.

Well, centre-half, perhaps, in the Liverpool team that had just added the FA Cup to its trophy cabinet. The man who was managing that mighty side had concluded that

I wasn't even going to be good enough to play for Huddersfield Town. That same man had left school at 14 to go down the pit. Yet he'd also seen something in me that a trained and apparently revered head teacher had not.

Viv had a job lined up in Peterborough as well. She'd recently left a red-brick university with a top qualification in social sciences. Now she had a very big challenge to look forward to as childcare officer for the social services department of Peterborough City Council.

Before moving to the flat that the community school had bequeathed to us in Glinton, there was the small matter of the honeymoon. Viv's Auntie Ella was going to let her have her house in Dover for a week. To say that I was looking forward to it was putting it mildly. With the speeches over, it would soon be time for the "happy couple" to make their excuses and leave, to coin a phrase apparently used by so-called investigative journalists in the News of the World. As an Observer reader, of course, I wouldn't have been seen dead with such a sordid "rag".

Viv had slipped away to change into what used to be called in those days the "going-away outfit". I couldn't wait to be with my bride on the first of two trains heading for the "Deep South". First there were prolonged farewells to family and friends followed by a short, chauffeured drive to Hereford Station.

We stood on the London-bound platform, alone at last. Or were we? Who was this coming towards us, waving wildly and smiling benignly?

No. Surely not. It couldn't be. Oh, yes, it was. I knew that "Auntie" Renee looked on me as the son she'd never had and made a big fuss of me on those Saturday-night card schools in our front parlour, but what was she doing heading for London on a Saturday afternoon? Surely she wasn't going to a gambling club in Soho.

Wherever she was going, she was sitting with us and seemed happy to jabber excitedly all the way. Viv was as diplomatic as ever, conversing politely when she could get the occasional word in. Much as I liked Auntie Renee, I was somewhat sullen. Couldn't help wondering whether my mother had set this up. Surely Renee wasn't coming with us all the way to Dover.

Mercifully, we parted company at Paddington. Can't for the life of me remember where she said she was going, probably because I didn't care. All I knew is that we were heading for Charing Cross.

Were there bluebirds over the white cliffs of Dover

when we finally arrived?

Didn't know. Didn't care about that either. I had only one thing on my mind as I carried my lovely bride over the threshold of Auntie Ella's edge-of-town house, serenaded by the raucous squawk and screech of seagulls at dusk.

The sun shone the following morning and continued to shine throughout that lovely week, as though promising us a bright future. We made all sorts of decisions. Not least which car Viv would buy. She needed one for her new job. British motor companies were in turmoil at the time and the Hillman Imp that we finally settled on was all-too-typically problematic. The water pump had to be changed about six times in the course of its comparatively short life.

Peterborough City Council had provided the loan to buy that little Imp. Unfortunately, however, they didn't run to funding mortgages for their employees. As a non-graduate teacher, I was paid just £9 a week. Viv earned slightly more, but not enough to impress the building societies. For a while at least we were going to be stuck in the one-roomed flat that the school had found for us in Ginton. One room, that is, plus a kitchen and bathroom shared with the landlady.

Thanks Shanks

Mrs Buck was a tartar with a cat to match. She and I took an instant dislike to one another. So did the cat and myself. An un-neutered tom, it hissed when anyone other than its mistress went anywhere near it, howled loudly through the night and dragged in rodents at regular intervals – particularly when it was our turn to use the kitchen.

The formidable Mrs Buck charged us £5 a week rent. Plus extras. A bar of soap was fourpence halfpenny, bearing in mind that the decimalisation of the currency was still six years away. Two gallons of oil for the heater was four shillings and fourpence. Admittedly that wouldn't have been much more than 20p in "new money", but those extras on top of the rent were taking a fair old bite out of my meagre wages.

No matter. We were young. We were married. We were happy. Well, I certainly was and, when she wasn't trying to ease tensions between myself, Mrs Buck and her cat, Viv gave the impression that she was happy too. As happy, that is, as any social worker in the harrowing speciality of childcare could be.

And my own job?

Well, I'll never forget that first day. As I strode to the school past unfamiliar flat fields with expansive skies overhead, that hissing cat would be quickly forgotten. I was about to meet the "Fenland Tigers".

Thanks Shanks

```
Rooms.              £ 5 · 0 · 0
milk          5·6
Laundry       3·0
Electric fr   2-0
gam
Sugar 2lb.    1-3
Soap            4½
Tea ½lb.      2· 6
            ─────────
            14· 7½
Collection     6
            ─────────
            15· 1½
```

Pear for Vivian to take
in morning

Dear Vivian,

I really must ask you
both to get in all your
baths etc before 9·30 pm
or anything whereby you can
make a noise. I was awakened
3 times last night just as
I was going off to sleep
& this morning my head was
bad till 2 pm. after lunch.
this cant go on please respect
my wishes

152

CHAPTER FOURTEEN

Taming the Tigers and Gaining Respect

It would be a gross exaggeration to suggest that I was about to enter a "blackboard jungle". The Fenland Tigers were simply kids from some 15 villages sprawled out under those wide open skies. There were 20 buses rounding them up every morning and bringing them into school. Reluctantly in many cases. They came from the land and they wanted to go back to the land where they could earn some money. Their expectations, in other words, were about as low as the horizon hereabouts. Cambridge University might as well have been a million miles away rather than just across the Fens.

The "Tigers" nickname had been bestowed by world-weary teachers who had occasionally been confronted by youths who had gained in muscle, if not brainpower, by spending every spare moment working on their fathers' farms. They could be quite aggressive, I'd been warned. Not as aggressive as some of the centre-forwards I'd encountered in my Huddersfield days, I told myself as I walked up one of the school's highly polished corridors with my mentor Ian Bedwell. "There you are," he smiled, coming to a sudden halt, "your class." He gestured at the door before scurrying off.

Determined to look formidable rather than tentative, I went through it with a stroll that verged on a swagger. To my great surprise, the entire class stood up immediately and chorused, "Good morning, Sir." As Tigers went, they were only cubs – first-years, as we called them in those days. After introducing myself as their form-tutor, I laid down a few basic ground rules, took the register and found out a bit about each of them.

So far so good.

After 20 minutes or so, I was off to deliver my first RE lesson with some fifth-formers in their mid-teens. They stood up as well, albeit somewhat less enthusiastically. And as soon as they clattered back into their desks, there was an outbreak of murmuring and giggling. It was my first day, after all, and I was going to talk about matters spiritual. Perhaps they thought I was going to be a benevolently easy touch.

If so, they were in for a surprise. I threw back my shoulders and stood up to my full height before targeting one lad who seemed to be giggling more than most. "You boy," I bellowed, "come here."

Taming the Tigers and Gaining Respect

No, I wasn't going to "cut the hide off him" like Frank Ball, that sadistic head teacher who had terrified us at Wibsey School in Bradford. Ball's viciousness was so etched into my memory that I'd vowed to myself never to resort to corporal punishment. Instead I told the giggling Tiger in no uncertain terms, "You don't do that in my lessons. If you do it again, there'll be serious consequences at the end of the day." Detention, in other words, which meant keeping him off the land even longer. And maybe making him miss his school bus, which meant that an irate parent would have to come and pick him up.

Whatever went through his head, it shut the boy up. And that went for the rest of the class. They seemed suddenly keen to hear about certain aspects of the Bible. So far so much better. What's more, it was about to get better still as PE took over from RE.

I was down on the timetable to do "double games" with three or four classes of fifth-formers. Not alone, I hasten to add. The head of PE was there as well and we split the group between us. "Right," I said to my group, "it's the first day of term so let's warm up with a game of football." And, yes, I joined in. Showed off a bit, to be honest, but it seemed to work. I did a couple of tricks and then nearly burst the net with a shot. Mouths were agape. I had a sudden fleeting memory of the reaction of spectators and team-mates when Denis Law first soared over a centre-half in his own much more illustrious Huddersfield days.

It would be an exaggeration to say that the Tigers had become pussy-cats, but those present seemed impressed. And word soon spread, like a rumble in the jungle. I had respect from then on.

Being young, idealistic and full of energy, I started a number of after-school activities, including the introduction of the Duke of Edinburgh Award scheme. Those who didn't have to rush off to catch buses to distant Fenland farms were taking part with a commitment almost bordering on enthusiasm.

Less enthusiastic, however, were some of my more senior colleagues in the staffroom. Snide comments suggested that I was seen as an upstart "smarty-pants" raising expectations among the farm-labouring classes. "David, I know you're keen but take it easy," the deputy head Frank Judd boomed at me in his broad Lancashire accent after taking me to one side for what turned out to be an anything-but-confidential chat. "You'll burn yourself out, lad, and you've got a lot of years to do yet."

He made it sound like a prison sentence. After a while, I went back and talked to him in what I hoped was a calm, quiet and reasonably polite way. "Look," I said, "I took note of what you said but, if you don't mind me saying so, I think you're wrong. It's a great privilege to be a teacher and we ought to take every opportunity to influence these young people. A good way of doing it is to give them extra opportunities."

"Here endeth the lesson," I might have added but didn't. Judd just smiled in a patronising way.

I got on far better with the head than his deputy. Initially at least. Jim Harvey gave me a performance-management report at the end of my first year which suggested that I'd passed with flying colours. I'd like to have been as complimentary about him as he was about me, but Jim had been at Glinton a long time and had become a bit complacent. At times it seemed more like a holiday camp than a school. "Can I take on any extra responsibilities?" I asked him at the beginning of the second year.

"Oh yes," he said vaguely. "Come and see me at Christmas and I'll try to find something for you." Christmas was at least nine weeks away and that seemed like a lifetime to me. But then something happened that would transform my life. Again.

Like Frank Judd, Wilf Wood was a Lancastrian with typically monosyllabic Christian and surnames. And, like Frank, he had been deputy head at Glinton. Still had a house in the school grounds, in fact. Disillusioned with the complacency of the place, he had taken on a headship at Walton, a tough school in Peterborough.

For some reason he had come home earlier than usual one day and, over the garden fence, he'd spotted this young and enthusiastic PE teacher running an after-school club. At Glinton! Whatever next? Who was this guy?

He sent his wife to find out. "My husband is a head teacher at the school down the road," Kathleen Wood had confided. "Would you mind giving him a ring?" With which she slipped a piece of paper into my hand. The suggestion of subterfuge was quite exhilarating. Protocol apparently dictated that a head teacher didn't want to be spied trying to poach a budding recruit, particularly from the school that was still granting him a grace-and-favour home.

It wasn't the first time that I'd been made an offer from the touchline of a football pitch. But this particular offer would prove to be rather more rewarding in the long-term. When I rang the number, the redoubtable Wilf laced temptation with flattery. "I watched you inspiring those kids," he said, "and I thought you were brilliant. Would you mind coming round to our house one evening? And perhaps you'd like to bring your wife with you."

No food was forthcoming. Just as well, perhaps, for someone weaned on brisket. Wilf and Kathleen were vegetarians. Teetotallers too. That didn't bother us. We had what used to be called a "coffee evening", and with the coffee came the offer to visit Walton and see what he was trying to do with the place.

I was flattered when he offered me a job just over 12 months after I'd taken my first step into teaching. Even better, there would be more money and more responsibility as head of PE. There was just one problem. I would have to tell Jim Harvey. When I did, he was surprisingly animated. Went berserk, you might say. He knew immediately that Wilf Wood was behind it, having been made well aware of Wilf's frustration with his own failure to move with the times. But it was me on whom he vented his own frustration. Have you no principles?" he thundered.

"Yes. I have a lot," I assured him. Then he calmed

down a bit and offered me more money. Principled as I was, it didn't take me long to turn it down and tell him that I was still determined to go to Walton.

Harvey made my life hell while I served my compulsory three months notice. He used to challenge everything I said in staff meetings and, on one occasion, he sent me to buy flowers for his secretary, as though I was a messenger boy.

Walton was a tough school in the middle of Peterborough. Around 60 per cent of the pupils were the children of Italian brick-workers – formidably powerful figures, for the most part, who didn't want anybody imposing discipline on their little "bambinos". I had a terrifying encounter with one brick-like brick-maker as I led an all-night cross-country hike to Stamford as part of the Duke of Edinburgh Award qualification. One of the girls, it seems, hadn't told her "Papa" where she was going. On being informed by his wife at the end of a lengthy shift, he had dived back into his car and come looking for us.

The headlights sliced through the enfolding darkness as he screeched to a halt on a narrow and deserted lane. He was a big man. Very big and very threatening as he stormed across the field, gesticulating wildly and uttering what sounded like insults in his native tongue. Without further ado, he came up to me, grabbed be by the lapels and hurled me into the nearest dyke. And, as you may have gathered, I was no lightweight. Clambering damply from the depths of the dyke, I did my best to appear unconcerned as the other children looked on with a mixture of astonishment and bafflement. The big man's daughter was sobbing as Papa led her back to the car with a protective arm around her shoulder, still looking back over his own shoulder every now and then to hurl incomprehensible insults in my direction.

Once the car had driven off, I was determined to reassert some dignity. My colleagues agreed. The dyke-hike would go on. My boots squelched for many a mile and my clothes had just about dried out by the time we reached Stamford.

Back at school, I was still pulling on my football boots at regular intervals. Even the Italian kids seemed to be impressed with my ball skills. Less so with my determination to keep them behind after school if they misbehaved. But I stuck to my guns and I had the feeling that I was making an impression in the classroom as well as in the gym and on the playing fields.

Wilf certainly seemed to think so. He soon made me

head of humanities, which meant an increase in salary on top of the £500-plus bonus that he'd secured for me when I'd first moved from Glinton. Then he said something that brought back echoes of Bill Shankly's astonishing suggestion that I really should be a teacher: "You really should be a head teacher."

Me? Who'd left school barely literate. Me? To whom maths remained an impenetrable puzzle? A head teacher?

No, I didn't have the necessary qualifications but – and this was beginning to sound very familiar – Wilf was going to help me. First of all, I needed a diploma in education and only one university offered a course that could fit in with my teaching commitments. Not Cambridge, needless to say. That would have been far too convenient. Instead I would have to drive to Nottingham two afternoons a week. And that was some 60 miles away. It was not going to be easy. Not for me. And not for Viv who had given birth to our first child Olwen in 1968, the year before I was due to start my bi-weekly travels. But there was at least one less frustration during our prolonged separation.

We no longer had to deal with Mrs Buck and her hissing cat.

CHAPTER FIFTEEN

Finding a Nest before Flying Away

It was just a bog-standard two-bedroom semi on a modern housing estate in the village of Northborough which, as the name suggests, was just north of Peterborough. The central heating was powered by a little coke boiler that proved extremely cantankerous and turned itself off at regular intervals. Bedroom floors seemed particularly chilly at times as we couldn't afford to carpet them or the stairs. After all, we'd had to lash out a hundred quid to acquire a dining table and some chairs to go round it.

To me, however, our new home seemed like a palace. I loved that long garden and the open-plan lounge, so different from the front parlour in Bradford. I loved the proximity of so many young couples who, like us, were getting their feet on the property ladder – a ladder that has been withdrawn from so many young couples today. I loved the fact that we'd finally said goodbye to the pernickety Mrs Buck and her wretched cat. But, above all, I loved the thought that this little corner of Cambridgeshire was ours. Technically, I suppose, it belonged to the building society but, thanks to Wilf Wood at Walton School, we had enough money to pay the mortgage.

Just about. Once we became parents, Viv wanted to stay at home to give Olwen the best start in life. Again that's an option denied to most young couples today. But our estate had a community of stay-at-home-Mums. Hopefully, I told myself, their presence would make my wife's life more bearable during my prolonged absences over the next couple of years or so.

The Hillman Imp had been replaced by a Vauxhall Victor, acquired from my father-in-law at a knock-down price, before I embarked on my lengthy journeys to Nottingham. Wilf had arranged the timetable so that I could slip out of Walton early on two afternoons a week, avoid the rush hour in Melton Mowbray and be at the university in time for the first lecture at 5pm. The roads were even less congested on those long journeys home with the headlights on full- beam for much of the way as main roads gave way to Fenland lanes.

I'd usually be back in Northborough by 10 and enjoy an undisturbed sleep, for the most part, despite a voluble toddler occupying the bedroom next door. Again that was down to Viv. It was she who got up when Olwen let rip in the middle of the night. I can't ever remember walking around with her in my arms, trying to get her to shut up and nod off. And although we had two more children and fostered even more, eventually, I'm ashamed to say that I've never changed a nappy in my life.

My sons despair of me. Women will mark me down as what they used to call a male chauvinist pig. All I can say in my defence is that I was a northern man of my times. Feminism was still in its infancy in 1969, the last year of a decade that had witnessed massive social change in other respects. University campuses were still hotbeds of political thought that was not just left of centre but outside-left, to coin a term that was no longer used in football.

University Park, Nottingham, was extensive and impressive. Awe-inspiring to somebody from my background. Two miles or so from the city centre, the vast and verdant campus had been laid out around a large lake during the inter-war years. The Portland Building, with its pillared portals, was particularly "awesome", as the youngsters say today. Like much else on the site, it was paid for by what D.H. Lawrence called the "shrewd cash-chemistry" of "good Sir Jesse Boot".

Thanks Shanks

Heaven knows what the Nottingham-born founder of Boots the Chemist would have made of some of the conversations that I overheard in the Student Union canteen when we were granted a brief break from lectures and debates around 6.30. Had he not died while Stalin's purges were just getting into their stride, Sir Jesse might have learnt something about the virtues of Ho Chi Minh and Chairman Mao. Not to mention the vices of those "union-bashers" in Downing Street and the "useless thickoes" running Nottingham City Council.

The canteen was buzzing in the early evening. We diploma-seeking teachers found a table tucked away in the corner, acutely conscious of our ties and sports jackets amid the abundance of faded denim, long hair and extremely short skirts. Sometimes, I admit, those skirts made it difficult to concentrate while some lecturer was languidly holding forth on the anti-bourgeois stance of Jean-Paul Sartre with the air of one lounging outside a cafe on Paris's Left Bank.

As canteens go, this one was positively exotic – and not just because of the clientele. No, it wasn't as imposing as the Three Counties Hotel in Hereford, where we'd had our wedding reception, or indeed that beamed-and-brassed pub in Ripon where I'd tucked into steak and chips on the way back from Roker Park. But there was so much choice. I sampled a pizza for the first time in my life. Liked it, too. There were curries as well. I'd never grown to like them, mind you, despite being a Bradford lad who'd also lived in Handsworth.

Perhaps because I'd seen at first-hand what life was like for so many poor people of all races in the back streets of Birmingham and Bradford, I became increasingly irritated by some of the political clap-trap that we heard during those brief breaks. It was obvious that some of the loudest advocates of working-class rights had come from a privileged middle-class background to this leafy, lake-side enclave sealed off from the real world. I doubted that they'd even ventured a mile or so down the road to Radford, a grim network of grimy terraced streets that had once been home to Alan Sillitoe. He was the author of *Saturday Night and Sunday Morning*, one of those gritty novels that had been all the rage in the previous decade before being turned into a grainy film of the "kitchen-sink" variety.

I may have been a fleeting bi-weekly visitor to Nottingham, but it quickly became apparent that the so-called "Queen of the Midlands" had some of the worst housing conditions in the country. The Meadows sounded delightful. It was anything but. As for St Ann's, it had been described as "a slum which crawls wearily over more than 300 of Nottingham's dirtiest acres". By Ken Coates and Bill Silburn, as it happened, two academics from the university's Adult Education Department. One of our own course lecturers took us on a visit there, by which time some of those stinking slums were finally being replaced by council houses with bathrooms and inside toilets. We also went to The Meadows which, at that time, remained largely unchanged – a blight on the south side of the city and a stark contrast with upmarket West Bridgford on the other side of the Trent.

The appalling conditions that we'd witnessed made me even more determined to speak out when some pumped-up windbag talked earnestly about "ordinary people" while holding forth in the canteen. "That's appalling," I growled. "You don't know anything about how ordinary people live." He looked a bit taken aback. So did those seated around him. Who was this short-haired Tyke in a tie?

Eventually, however, my increasingly regular interventions led to some animated debates. I enjoyed them. And I think some of the students enjoyed them too. Not too sure about my fellow-diploma-seekers. They kept looking at their watches pointedly as those pizza-and-politics discussions threatened to grind on beyond break-time.

That was the last thing I wanted. Heaven knows, I needed to make the most of my unexpected opportunity. So I'd take the hint and follow them back to the Education Department. There we had all sorts of debates about equality of opportunity. Sometimes I'd mention what I'd just heard in the Student Union canteen and the tutor would encourage me. The awe that had slightly intimidated me at my first glimpse of the campus had disappeared. I was becoming more outspoken as well as better at writing. Essays had to be done at weekends. More thoughts about issues such as leadership and the politics of education; even less time with the family.

Still, I finished that course with a distinction. Another one! And that proved invaluable in my quest for the masters degree that I would need to become a head-teacher. Wilf had managed to swing me a one-year secondment on full salary. Now I could apply to the only university in the country that would accept applicants for the MA without an honours degree. A diploma with a distinction was enough to get me into Lancaster for the 1971-72 academic year.

Thanks Shanks

In the meantime, our second child Matthew had been born. His presence made us feel even more blessed as a family. It also made our forthcoming temporary separation even more painful. Lancaster was over 200 miles away, which made Nottingham seem like a hop, skip and a jump. Never mind two nights a week; I was going to be away for two weeks at a time. Admittedly the terms were only 10 weeks long with lengthy "vacations" in between. All the same, it wasn't going to be easy for Viv.

Or me for that matter. Lancaster was one of the "new" universities that had been built in the 1960s and, in the spirit of that decade, it offered a goodly percentage of places to the offspring of families that had never sent anyone into higher education before. Yet it was run on a collegiate basis, like Oxford and Cambridge. I found myself in Cartmel College, in a room very similar to the one I'd had at St Peter's – desk, single bed and not much else.

There was a communal bathroom down the corridor and a phone box nearby. Every evening I pumped it with a succession of those new-fangled 5p pieces, which were the same size as the shillings they'd replaced. I felt lonely and homesick and desperately needed to talk to Viv.

Finding a Nest before Flying Away

Needless to say, she put on a brave voice, whether or not Olwen or Matthew, or both, had kept her up half the night.

The coursework was far more demanding than its equivalent on the Nottingham diploma. But at least it kept me fully occupied. Particularly the statistics. Yes, the anathema of maths had come back to haunt me. This time I was determined to overcome it. Luckily, there were two or three colleagues on the course who went out of their way to help me.

One of them was also good enough to give me a lift down the M6 every other Friday and on to the M1 before dropping me at one of the junctions. Viv, who had the Vauxhall while I was away, would drive over with the kids and pick me up. That was the idea. The first of such liaisons, however, proved to be a farcical misunderstanding worthy of an Ealing comedy. Carry On Past the Junction perhaps.

Somehow there had been a misunderstanding on a crackly phone line. I was waiting for her at junction 17 and she was waiting for me at junction 16. Or it may have been the other way around. Time passed. Panic mounted. No mobile phones in those days, needless to say. To cut a very long story short, we had an emotional

171

reunion two or three hours later in the unromantic setting of a local bus station.

Those weekends when I had to stay in Lancaster seemed to go on forever. Yes, I had essays to write and statistics to grapple with. But there had to be some down-time and, unlike my fellow course members, I didn't particularly want to spend that time in the bar. I'd never acquired a taste for alcohol any more than I had for curry. Not for the first time, I found refuge and friendship in the Methodist Society.

There was one weekend when, instead of me going home to the family, the family came to see me. Not in Lancaster but just up the road. What could be nicer than a spending time at the seaside?

Just about anything rather than a day in Morecambe. I've heard that it's improved a lot recently, but in those days it made Mablethorpe seem like a resort on the Cote d'Azur. This was a place that had seen better days. It seemed run-down, with a lot of empty boarding houses, amusement arcades that were anything but amusing and fairground attractions that were not in the least attractive. Viv disliked it even more than Bradford. When the tide went out, the sea seemed to disappear almost completely, leaving a sealed-off pool for the kids to paddle in. Despite prolonged protests from Olwen, her mother wasn't going to let them anywhere near it. The water was filthy.

We weren't sorry to say goodbye to Morecambe. And I would soon be bidding farewell to Lancaster. There would be one last visit, however. As well as Viv and the children, Mum and Dad came with me. They wanted to see their lad – the one they just wanted to be happy – receiving a scroll in the Great Hall while swathed in a black gown.

Happy? You bet I was. Despite my statistical night-mare, that precious MA was mine. I was thankful, too. Thankful to Viv for her unwavering support, thankful to Wilf Wood for making it possible, thankful to my tutors at St Peter's and to Steve Allott who done so much to ease my passage into teacher-training college.

None of that would have happened without Bill Shankly's perception and money. He'd been over the moon, as they say in football, when I'd told him that I'd scraped through in O-level English. Heaven knows how he'd have reacted if I could have told him that I now had a masters degree and was on my way to becoming a head-teacher.

At the time, I suspected, he had other things on his

mind. Liverpool had finished third at the end of the 1971-72 season, behind Don Revie's Leeds and Brian Clough's Derby County. Only just, mind you. In a dramatic end to the season, Leeds had lost 2-1 at Wolves and Liverpool could have won the title were it not for Arsenal's rugged back four holding out for a nil-nil draw at Highbury. Somehow they had denied Liverpool's latest human dynamo from scoring, despite a valiant effort on his part.

Shankly had signed Kevin Keegan from Scunthorpe the previous year for just £35,000. That was £20,000 below Denis Law's transfer fee to Manchester City a decade previously. Keegan would go on to play a major part in Liverpool landing the League and the UEFA Cup the following season before establishing himself as an Anfield legend and a highly regarded England international.

Proof, if any more was needed, that Shankly always could spot a good 'un'.

CHAPTER SIXTEEN

Sending Ourselves to Coventry

I had been warned. An excitable junior teacher had just burst into my office to tell me that a parental threat was advancing on the school. "His wife's just rung up to warn us," he stuttered. "And I've just seen him striding up the drive. Blimey, he's a big guy. He's got a t-shirt with no sleeves and tattoos all over his arms. Big boots as well. With red laces," he added after a pause for dramatic effect.

Not just a skinhead then, but more than likely a member of the National Front. That loathsome racist rabble of a populist party was riding a wave of support in major industrial cities by the mid-1970s.

A sudden commotion in the secretary's office heralded the Big Guy's arrival. "Where's Kershaw?" he bawled. I opened my door and my colleague somehow slipped away.

Alone then. Throwing back my shoulders, I tried to assert the "presence" that had served me so well on the football field. "I'm David Kershaw," I confirmed. "Would you mind coming into my office, Mr So-and-so." Yes, he was a so-and-so and, no, I can't remember his real name.

What I will never forget is his forehead. It too was tattooed. Low as it was, the message inscribed across that furrowed brow was all too clear and all too repellent: "I hate n******". There were no asterisks, however. The n-word was written out in full. Which put his daughter's behaviour into perspective. She was 14, adept at telling teachers where to go, prolific with the "f" word and, earlier that day, she had turned up with her lengthy locks covered in some garish dye. A deliberately provocative act, I'd concluded, and sent her home after checking that someone was in. The mother had been quite apologetic over the phone. "It was a mistake," she assured me. "We'll get it sorted."

Her other half seemed more intent on getting me "sorted". My intention had been to get him to sit down and calm down so that we could have some kind of discussion. But that tattooed message had crossed a line and not just a furrow. "I'm sorry," I blurted, "but every bit of my being feels that what's written on your forehead is wrong. No, it's not just wrong; it's evil. And you're going to leave or I'll ring the police."

He came round the desk and lunged at me. Almost took off. Luckily those boots obeyed the law of gravity and kept part of him carpet-bound. I was still quite nifty on my feet and managed to skirt round the other side of the desk. While he was on the floor, I was out of the door, locking it behind me.

The police came quickly. Not quickly enough, however, to stop that so-and-so from causing considerable damage to my office furniture with his red-laced size elevens. It suddenly seemed a long time since I'd expressed a wish to get back into the "rough-and-tumble" of school life after a couple of years lecturing at the Coventry College of Education. The college was based in the suburb of Canley, not far from Alderman Callow School where I was now deputy head.

At the heart of Canley was a large council estate and the school was situated at the far end, close to the A45. That road was, and still is, a busy four-lane highway with London signposted one way, Birmingham the other and a different world on its far side. There lay Warwick University which, despite its name, was within the boundaries of Coventry. Just about. There also was Cannon Park, one of the city's more upmarket addresses, its tree-lined roads harbouring large houses, expansive gardens and expensive cars.

They made cars in Canley. Many of the houses on the

estate were occupied by those who worked on the track at nearby Standard-Triumph, or in factories elsewhere in the city that would be closing down all too soon. What appealed to me about working at Alderman Callow was the opportunity it offered to try to bridge the gap between Canley and Cannon Park. After all, that was why we'd come to Coventry in the first place. It was leading the way in eliminating the divisions put between children at the age of 11 by the grammar-and-secondary-modern system. My own personal experience of those divisions had left its mark and I was passionately committed to the comprehensive cause.

John Rennie, one of our lecturers at Nottingham University, worked in Coventry as adviser for community education. He'd told me that the local authority there was also staunchly committed to giving parents and other local residents the opportunity to become more involved in school life. That appealed to me as well. Glinton had whetted my appetite for community education. Now there beckoned the historic city that had risen from the ruins of the Blitz and reinvented itself as the forefront of modernity. Coventry had begun to sound like Shangri-La.

Needless to say, it didn't prove to be an earthly paradise and my later experience with the tattooed racist would show me that there was another side to parental involvement. But I've never regretted upping sticks and moving from the Fenlands to the Midlands, even if it did take us rather a long time to find a house. Coventry was still something of a boom-town at the time. Its long tradition of attracting workers from around Britain, Ireland and beyond had, it seemed, been interrupted only briefly by its war-time horrors.

To stand a chance of finding a three-bedroom semi we'd have to be at the first estate agent's office by nine am. Not easy when we had two children, another on the way and had to drive nigh-on 70 miles. The agent might give us three addresses. Each would be gone by the time we arrived. It was particularly galling when one house was almost next door to a Methodist church. That would have been very handy. On another occasion, we arrived at the property at 10 am to find no fewer than five potential buyers in front of us.

So we finished up living in nearby Rugby, which seemed small and parochial. What's more, it harboured a renowned public school that charged extraordinary fees to super-rich parents to buy a privileged education for their offspring. Occasionally you'd see those uniformed fellows swanning around town in straw-boaters. Their insouciance only confirmed my faith in improving the lot of children from backgrounds such as my own.

Before getting the chance to be back at the sharp end of comprehensive education, however, I would have to give lectures on its aims and principles. It was John Rennie who had persuaded me to apply for the job at the Coventry College of Education. "If you went there for a couple of years," he'd said, "you could help us get the university on side and see what's happening in a number of Coventry schools."

Wilf Wood had offered no objections. Pleased as punch about my MA, which he had made possible, he'd waived my obligation to do three months notice and let me leave my job at Walton School in September, 1972. His final words to me had been "Don't let me down, David. You're going to be a head one day."

As it turned out, the College of Education didn't become part of Warwick University until 1978, by which time I'd long since left to clamber aboard the penultimate step on the ladder to headship. My big chance had come when a big man with a big, booming Yorkshire voice had begun to make his presence felt in the corridors around the lecture theatre. Mike Frost – or Doctor Michael Frost, to give him his full title – had been head of President Kennedy, Coventry's biggest school with some 2,000 pupils. He was 6ft 4 inches tall, broad of shoulder and ample of girth. What's more, he was going to be head of Alderman Callow, the new school designed to unite the disparate communities of Canley and Cannon Park. While the building was nearing completion, he had been found a temporary office in our college.

Mike came from York originally. So we'd talk about cricket and about life from a Yorkshire point of view. We'd also talk about education. And it didn't take long for him to pinpoint me as the one he wanted to be his deputy head. "You'll have to go through the process," he'd confided in a voice that could have been heard in Rugby. "But I want your enthusiasm. And you need to get back into schools."

Too right. I couldn't wait for my interview. Until, that is, I saw the person ahead of me emerge from the room in the Council House looking shattered, as though he'd been through a particularly fierce grilling. He was shaking as he grabbed hold of the banister rail on the landing and looked for a moment as though he was going to hurl himself over it. I was trying to think of something sympathetic to say when the door opened and a disembodied voice rang out from within. "Mr Kershaw, can you come in, please?"

There were two men in there and they might as well have been labelled Mr Nice and Mr Nasty, an interviewing technique used by the police. Or so I'm told. Bob Aitken, the Director of Education who had a national reputation, was lounging in his chair and beaming amicably. Next to him was Councillor Peter Lister, chairman of the Education Committee, who looked distinctly stern. Not unusually so, as I would later discover. A formidable figure in local government, he would eventually become a respected leader of the City Council. But it's fair to say that he didn't suffer fools gladly. In his obituary in The Guardian in 2002, a fellow Labour councillor described him as "difficult with opponents and impossible with his friends".

Now here he was, just across the table from me and waiting to be unleashed. "Peter," Bob Aitken breezed, "here's a young man who, I'm told, has lots of ideas. But he needs testing. Over to you."

Lister gave me a blistering look before launching into the first part of the test. "Imagine you've been appointed to Alderman Callow in Canley," he said. "I know Canley. Some rough diamonds live there. Tough families. What are you going to do on your first day when a mother comes in and tells you to 'piss off'?"

There were more questions like that and I must have made a reasonable fist of answering them because, eventually, he turned to Aitken and said with a nod, "Okay, take him on now."

Really? Did that mean I'd got the job? Not quite. The Director of Education proceeded to take me on with a series of questions. Luckily, I felt completely at ease while answering them. And, as you well know, I did get the job and I enjoyed it for the most part. One of my roles was to devise a curriculum. Remember this was still a few years before central government began to impose its restrictive demands on schools. Apart from English, Maths, Science, History and Geography, we made a big thing of sport in its widest context and well as the performing arts. Plus Spanish, which was slightly easier than French and certainly one more foreign language than kids from secondary-modern schools would have been taught.

Long hair was fashionable at the time. Sometimes I felt a bit like a sergeant-major going round and telling boys to "get it cut". Apart from anything else, dangling strands could be a liability in PE and design technology classes.

Such was my reputation for imposing discipline that I became known in the playground as "killer Kershaw". And that, in turn, had led to a least one parent trying to kill me – or at least trying to give me a good kicking. It was only when Canley parents felt that their little darlings were being unfairly chastised that they turned up to complain or tell me to "piss off". Like my own Mum and Dad, they were very reluctant to engage with the school in a positive way. Yet we were supposed to be leading the way in community as well as comprehensive education. How were we going to encourage that engagement?

Canley had one of many thriving working men's clubs in Coventry and we set up meetings in the committee room once a month, on a Thursday evening. My colleagues would be nursing pints, including Mike Frost who had reacquainted himself with Tetley's Bitter, albeit out of a tank rather than a barrel. The idea was to show people that we weren't snooty academics. We were accessible, open to suggestions. Often we'd start with a discussion about rent arrears and housing issues before dropping in items about education.

Only half a dozen club members came at first but word

seemed to get around. Eventually the room was full. Local councillors came along. So did women, which was quite an advance. The name "working men's club" spoke for itself. Female members seemed to be tolerated rather than welcomed in those days. Only in certain parts of the building, I might add. The snooker room, for instance, was hallowed male turf – or rather baize.

We'd also hold regular gatherings at Cannon Park Primary School between five and seven pm. Parents would call in on their way home from work. For the most part, they had one question that they wanted answering: "Can you guarantee that our children are not going to be bullied by those nasty thugs from Canley?"

We assured them that we'd be keeping a close eye on what went on in the playground as well as in the corridors. After all, these were middle-class people with the luxury of choice. Some would try to get their children into Finham Park on the other side of the Kenilworth Road. Others might try Kenilworth itself, which was only a couple of miles away. Those with money to spare could pay for their children to "go private", as two of the city's former grammar schools were now charging fees.

So were we wasting our time by trying to link these very different communities on either side of the A45?

Thanks Shanks

Hardly. We needed to have an annual intake of 180 children. There were just 50 in the first year but we were full by the time I left in 1980. Mike Frost was leaving too. Wanted to move back "oop North" apparently.

Not me. I was still committed to Coventry. Apart from, anything else, I'd finally found us a house. After one of those parents' meetings in Cannon Park, I'd turned left off the A45 towards the centre of town. The Kenilworth Road at this point is a glorious gateway to a city centre, bordered as it is by dense woodland with the vast Memorial Park to the right and the sought-after suburb of Earlsdon to the left. On a whim I turned left and then left again, into the aptly named Woodland Avenue. And there it was: a for sale sign on a semi-detached built sometime between the wars. No queue of would-be buyers outside, what's more. I rang the estate agent first thing in the morning and managed to buy the place for £14,600.

Viv and I have lived there ever since. Children have flown the nest, coming back at regular intervals with grandchildren. The house has been much extended and the mortgage paid off. None of which I could have imagined back then at the beginning of a turbulent decade that would be defined by the dominant politician of the day, one Margaret Thatcher.

Briefly, and most uncharacteristically, there was also a Conservative City Council in power in Coventry. They'd been elected in 1978 at a time when the Labour Government was in the depths of its unpopularity and there loomed what Jim Callaghan called a "sea-change in politics".

My quest for a headship hit a temporary setback when I turned up for another interview at the Council House to find myself confronted by all 25 members of the Education Committee. I thought I'd performed reasonably well in the circumstances. The Tories who dominated that committee evidently thought differently. To them I was almost certainly too young, too radical, too northern and too left-wing.

Bob Aitken called me into his office soon after my rejection was confirmed. "David," he said, "I'm devastated. We live in Cannon Park and, as you know, I sent my son to Alderman Callow because I believe in what you're doing there." Then he paused before telling me that there was another job coming up for a head teacher. "I want you to apply for it." Another pause, "Although it might be challenging."

I was about to find out why.

Thanks Shanks

CHAPTER SEVENTEEN

Gaining Promotion and Heading for the Top

Once again I found myself in Coventry's imposing council chamber being interrogated by the entire Education Committee. It didn't seem five minutes since the last time. There had been one fundamental change, however. Labour had taken back control of the local authority.

There were five of us up for the headship of Coundon Court - a surprisingly high number of candidates for a school with such a poor reputation. Two of my rivals already had experience as head teachers elsewhere. That didn't bode well. Nor had my mother's reaction to the revelation that I'd grown a beard. "He'll never get promotion with whiskers round his chops," she'd told Viv with grave foreboding on one of our increasingly cramped weekends with the Bradford branch of the family.

As it turned out, Mum was proved wrong. It was me who was summoned back into the council chamber at the end of the interview process. Me who was told by the chairman of the Education Committee, one Councillor

Thanks Shanks

Harry Richards, that I was to be the new head of Coundon Court. Me: the one with the beard. Me: the one who had been told by his own head teacher that he wasn't very bright.

That would have been 24 years previously. It was now January, 1981. I was 38 and about to become the youngest person ever to take over the headship of a senior school in Coventry. Yes, of course I was proud. Elated too. Not quite as elated as Mum when I rang to tell her and she almost screamed with joy. Wilf Wood didn't scream, but his delight was all too evident when I phoned the school in Peterborough to confirm that his faith in my leadership qualities had finally been rewarded.

Bill Shankly would also have been delighted, I suspect. He'd retired in 1974 and, by all accounts, had more than enough time on his hands to reflect on the past. I should have made more of an effort to find a forwarding address and tell him what a difference his perception and money had made to my life. But I didn't. It wasn't just that I was busy and about to become busier still. There was also an element of shame. As a proud and cussed Yorkshireman, it was a step too far to admit that I'd needed so much help to get on the ladder. So I'd never talked about it, at college or at any of the schools were I'd worked. It seemed like a weakness and I didn't like to accept weakness in myself.

There are times, though, when the past comes rushing back on an unexpected tide of emotion. And I don't mind admitting that it hit me full in the face when news of Shankly's sudden death came through only just over six months after I'd become a head teacher. Without him I might still have been stacking shelves at Marks and Spencer's or become just another mill-worker facing redundancy. Jobs had been disappearing in the Yorkshire woollen world long before the collapse of Coventry's car factories.

At least I had a job. A hell of a job as it turned out. My predecessor as head of Coundon Court had resigned a year earlier and gone back to Birmingham. There were stories in the local press that Coundon parents were refusing to send their children to the school on their doorstep. As a temporary measure, Bob Aitken had appointed Mike Frost's successor at President Kennedy to try to bring some order out of chaos. Ken Reynolds had done his best during his 12 months in charge. He was a big, plain-speaking Australian and his last words to me were "I've just scratched the surface, mate. Best of luck."

We shook hands and off he went through the heavy,

elaborately decorated oak door of the head's office here in what was known as The Old House. It had been the home of George Singer, one of Coventry's many cycle manufacturers who had moved into motor cars towards the end of his life. The building that he'd bequeathed was a classic piece of late-Victorian architecture with a well-stocked library extending over four rooms with some elaborate oak-panelling. Even better, it was on the edge of the Wedge – a gently undulating spread of common land, lined with ancient hedges and mature trees, between the suburb of Coundon and the village of Allesley.

A splendid setting then for Coundon Court's administrative hub. But, alas, the more recent additions to the school site had not been built in such a stylish and formidable fashion. Most of them were thrown up under CLASP, otherwise known as the Consortium of Local Authorities' Special Programme. They were prefabricated, looked like Meccano and seemed to give a bit if you leaned on the sides. One of the blocks was a big, two-storey building and, apparently, quite an architectural feat when it was originally erected for the selective girls' school that had had the site all to itself until comparatively recently. Nice wide corridors and big classrooms, for sure. But, oh my goodness, the walls looked more like honeycombs. If you banged the plaster, it would give way to a hole. There were some of walls that were just holes with little else in between. Many a blazered elbow had been rammed into creating them.

As for the boys' toilets, they were disgusting. There wasn't one that worked properly. In some cases, whole cisterns had been wrenched off the walls. There was graffiti everywhere – racist stuff as well as crude sexual comments worthy of the Cleckheaton changing room in my Huddersfield Town days.

This place was going to make Alderman Callow seem like a dream school. There were almost 2,000 children from very diverse backgrounds. In its previous all-girls incarnation, Coundon Court had been overseen by a fearsome headmistress called Miss Foster who had insisted that the young ladies who crossed its threshold had two pairs of shoes: outdoor and indoor. It had been well disciplined with high academic standards. Among its alumni was Mo Mowlam whose later manifestation as Secretary of State for Northern Ireland oversaw the signing of the Good Friday Agreement of 1998.

Overseeing the comprehensive education system in Coventry, Bob Aitken had brought the Coundon girls together with the mixed but predominantly boys' school of Barker Butts, a mile or so down the road towards the city centre. Some of its pupils came from the inner-city, others from the large council estate of Radford. They were tough kids in many cases and the school had a reputation for producing top rugby players.

Unlike most cities and towns on this side of Offa's Dyke, Coventry didn't confine rugby union to its grammar and independent schools. That may well explain why Coventry RFC was such a formidable force in the English game until the coming of the professional era. Barker Butts was one of its prime feeder schools.

But I digress. If I was ever going to unite the youngsters from Barker Butts with the girls from Coundon Court, I needed a long-term plan. I also needed to get the teachers on my side.

Easier said than done. To say that I sensed hostility in some quarters was putting it mildly. At our first staff meeting some of the well-established "masters" from Barker Butts weren't so much testing as taunting me. To a man, they were staunch believers in corporal punishment. One of them even handed me a cane. I couldn't have looked more disapproving if he'd offered me a joint. "Are you one of those yellow-bellied liberals?" one of his colleagues sneered. "Because if you are, you'll fail." Knocking those troublesome kids into shape with a good thrashing was the only language they understood, apparently.

My memories of Frank Ball "cutting the hide off" that poor lad at Wibsey Secondary Modern in Bradford had left me with a lifelong hatred of corporal punishment. It was time to make that plain and assert my authority. In morning assembly I laid down the law as to what I believed in, conscious that one or two teachers were sniggering in the back row. Some of them behaved even worse than the boys who had, allegedly, been under their control.

Sifting out those sniggerers would take time. Local authorities had control over school budgets in those days, which meant that you couldn't just sack teachers and replace them with better ones. What you could do was make plain your plans to change the culture of the school, get a coterie of colleagues on your side and persuade them to share your vision of how the place could be transformed. Which was what I did. Eventually that is. But there were many more obstacles in the short-term – not least the combustible politics of the times.

The early years of Thatcherism were excessively

confrontational. Not least between her Government, with its underlying doctrine of monetarism, and the trade unions whose powers "the lady" seemed determined to curb at any cost. As president of the National Union of Teachers locally, I knew which side I was on.

Or did I?

Shortly after my arrival at Coundon Court, school cleaners and caretakers were called out on strike by NUPE, the National Union of Public Employees, as they were known before they evolved into UNISON. Our school was going to remain locked up, it seemed. But I wasn't having that. My first responsibility was to the children. So I approached the caretaker and persuaded him to hand over the keys.

That was the easy bit. Having parked the car outside the nearby Nugget pub, I walked on, walked on – not so much with hope in my heart as determination. I knew there'd be a NUPE picket line at the school gate. What I hadn't anticipated was the presence of so many supportive NUT members, from Coundon Court and elsewhere. One of them shouted out that I was "a northern mill-owner" as I ploughed on past the placard-wavers and cat-callers. Mill-owner? I didn't know whether to laugh or cry.

Gaining Promotion and Heading for the Top

I opened up The Old House and some 30 or so teachers turned up. That was out of a staff of nigh-on 200 full and part-timers. Still, I'd made my point. I was a person of conviction and I wasn't going to be intimidated by anyone. Teachers have rights and I'd be the first to defend that principle. But the rights of children to an education come ahead of everything else.

Needless to say, the NUT expected me to resign. And that's what I did, having been accused by the union of "joining the enemy". Some former members, long retired in most cases, still regard me as an enemy to this day. Yet I got on famously with John Haywood, the NUT rep at Coundon Court, once he'd accepted that he wasn't allowed to bring a tape recorder into our meetings. Indeed I had no problem with any of the unions in face-to-face meetings because I wanted to do things properly. First and foremost, however, my commitment was to raising standards for the students in our school.

Far too many of them had been written off as "thick". Bearing in mind my background, the word was like a red rag to a bull to me. My long-term plan involved developing a quality leadership team of around a dozen. We brought in a programme of professional development for every teacher. I made it plain to all staff members that lessons had to be properly prepared. Work had to be marked and children were not to be hit. The ultimate sanction for persistent reprobates was to be sent to my office. Slamming that huge oak door after they'd walked in had the desired effect of emphasising who was in charge. Then I'd give them a going-over — verbally, that is. "If you don't agree to this," I'd tell them, "I shall be on the phone to your parents. One of them [sometimes there was only one] will have to come and collect you. Then you'll have to come back to school and stay between four and five every evening to catch up on the work you've missed."

Nine times out of ten that worked a treat. Admittedly there were occasional confrontations with parents but, mercifully, not one of them was like the Canley skinhead with the low, tattooed forehead and the big boots. Getting parents on our side was a fundamental part of the plan. I was still committed to community as well as comprehensive education. We'd meet them informally, at the Nugget or the Coundon Social Club, which was rather more upmarket than its "working men's" equivalent in Canley. We'd invite them into the school — to take part in sixth-form classes, in some cases. And we'd get them involved in sporting activities, bearing in mind that some of our staff went along with the unions' work-to-rule that called on teachers not to take part in extra-curricular activities.

Sport had been a big part of my life, in and out of schools. I was determined to use it as a constructive part of an extended curriculum. My firm belief was that sport helped with disciplinary issues through the development of personal responsibility and, eventually, it encouraged youngsters to take pride in their school.

We built up the best school rugby team in the city. One of our prop forwards was Rob Hardwick, who went on to captain Coventry and play 167 times for London Irish. Even came on as a sub for England once in 1996. We also brought on Leon Lloyd who had an illustrious career as a back for Leicester Tigers.

As I may have mentioned, rugby was never really my game. Still, I made it my business to be on one touchline or another every Saturday morning, be it rugby, netball or hockey. Football, too. The round-ball was below the oval-ball in the school games pecking order but our head of English, Richard Hoare, had started a Coundon Court Old Boys XI that moved up relentlessly from division five to the top flight of the Coventry Alliance League. Me? I turned out a couple of times a year for the staff team. What I'd learnt from playing the game at a decent level offset the effect of advancing years and earned me some respect.

Although cricket was beginning its sad and slow decline in state schools, we had a team up and running under the redoubtable leadership of Steve Wilkes – another of our teachers and another stalwart of Coventry RFC. Indeed Steve had played for England and was only just coming to the end of his rugby career.

Back in the classrooms, meanwhile, those honeycombed walls had long-ago been covered by wood-panelling. The panels had, in turn, been covered by pictures – everything from David Hockney prints to geographical scenes and photographs of well-known sporting figures. There were no pictures in the boys' toilets, mind you, although the damaged cisterns had long been replaced and the graffiti removed. And, no, the vandalism had not made a comeback. Had it done so, the culprits would have been flushed out, as it were.

Her Majesty's Inspectors paid a visit about five years after I'd taken over. Fifteen of them came over a period of four days. One inspector or another would come back to my office at regular intervals and say that this was going well but that might need some tweaking. Substantial improvements had been made, they said in their report to the Education Committee and the school governors. There was, however, still some way to go.

And some way we went. Ofsted reports in the '90s regularly graded us as outstanding. By the turn of the century, if you please, we'd been classified as a "Beacon" and a "Talisman" school by the Department of Education. We seemed to have gone from being the worst-performing school in the city to the best. I had a lot of people to thank for that, not least my wife. Viv had been as supportive as ever, taking on the major role in ensuring that our own three children had a good education while I'd been so busy overseeing the education of others. She'd even found time to re-train as a teacher herself and take on a job in an inner-city primary school where her social-work skills came in very handy.

It was 2001 when I finally retired from Coundon Court. After 20 years in charge, it seemed like the right time to hand over to somebody else. It was also 20 years since the death of the legendary football manager who had seen something in me that my own head teacher had not.

Thanks, Shanks. But I wasn't finished in education yet. Not by a long way.

Thanks Shanks

POSTSCRIPT

It wasn't that 20 years seemed like a nice round figure and it was time to call it a day at Coundon Court. I loved the place and could happily have stayed on. After all, I was only 59. But the Department of Education had come-a-calling with an offer that was difficult to resist. They wanted me to sort out another failing school that Ofsted had decreed to be in "special measures". Not as a head teacher, mind you. No, I was going to be the Department's representative adviser.

Of all the education joints in all the towns in all of England, Bowling Secondary School just happened to be in inner-city Bradford. Yes, Bradford. Oh, the irony. Officials at the D of E had evidently heard about the transformation of Coundon Court, but I doubt that they knew of my origins in that city where I'd been written off aged 11 and 14.

Going back there was quite an emotional experience. No, I didn't stay in my old box-room, although the memories came flooding back as I drove north and checked into a hotel in the city centre. We'd bought the Horton Bank Top house for Dad a few years previously when the protected rent that he'd enjoyed for so many years was about to come to an end. Having to pay the market rate would have greatly distressed him. As it turned out, he died peacefully at home in 1999. By that time he was 90. My sister Ann, alas, was only 61 when the shocking news of her death came through from Geneva. Lung cancer, apparently, yet she was only an occasional smoker. What transpired from the inquest was that she had inhaled asbestos through cleaning out hair dryers at the salon where she'd worked in Leeds many years previously.

And Mum? Well, she had suffered a prolonged death from breast cancer back in 1980 when she was still in her 60s and treatments were nothing like as advanced as they are today. It was painful to watch her pain. We travelled up to visit her as often as possible during a prolonged process. By a cruel twist of fate, however, her beloved son wasn't there during her final hours. I wasn't at work either. We were away on a short family holiday. Why did that make me feel so guilty?

I didn't have too much time to reflect on that when I found myself back in Bradford 21 years after her death. There was work to be done. Only by being at my desk until 10 o'clock every evening did I manage to cram five days into four and be able to spend a long weekend at home in Coventry.

Postscript

Bowling School was out of special measures within two years and is now known as the Bradford Cathedral Academy. Mission accomplished? Not yet. Not by a long way. The D of E sent me to other schools in the city, including – irony of ironies – the one where I'd been told that I wasn't very bright (see Chapter Three). They also despatched me to Blackburn, Oldham and Liverpool as well as places closer to home: Leicester, Birmingham and Sandwell.

"Home" has long been Coventry, despite my inbuilt identity as a dyed-in-the-woollen-mill Yorkshireman. I wanted to make a further contribution to my adopted city so I stood in the local council elections of 2010. A vacancy had come up in the Bablake ward, hitherto a safe seat for the Conservatives. It included Coundon where many a voter had known me as a head of the local school. Only now could I let them know that I had been a lifelong member of the Labour Party.

Two years after my election, Ann Lucas became Council leader and asked me to take over as "cabinet lead" for education. Instead of waiting to be interviewed by the entire Education Committee, I was now chairing it. On the very week that I was appointed, Chief Inspector of Schools, Sir Michael Wilshaw, published a national report on primary education with the now obligatory league table. Coventry was bottom. Only 42 per cent of its primary schools were considered good or outstanding. Far too many were either in special measures or deemed to require improvement.

Enter Kirston Nelson as Director of Education, appointed by Chief Executive Martin Reeve and myself. Kirston and I got on well professionally, worked very closely with the city's heads and drove through the necessary changes. By the time I vacated the chair of the Education Committee in 2016, the number of good or outstanding primaries in Coventry had risen to 84 per cent – twice the figure from four years previously.

Viv's support had been steadfast as usual. Without her I could never have made a difference to the life-chances of so many children. As for our own children, well Olwen became a lawyer who still works for the Ministry of Justice in a senior role, Matthew is chief executive of a hospital trust in Kent and Richard is business manager of the Sidney Stringer Multi-Academy Trust, made up of four schools in central Coventry.

Between them they've blessed us with seven grandchildren and a surprising number of sporting memories. Olwen hated PE with a passion at school, yet she's run quite a few half-marathons since. Matthew has done at least six marathons and has even endured the Iron Man Triathlon, widely considered to be the most physically demanding one-day sporting event imaginable. As for Richard, he's a very useful batsman. Got a couple of hundreds last season, albeit in settings very different from the ones that his Dad remembers from the lower reaches of the Bradford League.

But then his Dad might – just might – have become a professional footballer. Instead of telling me that I wasn't going to make it, Bill Shankly could have said, "You really ought to be in the first team." Or better still, "You really ought to come with me to Liverpool." In my dreams, that is.

I'd have felt a lot better at the time. Over the moon, as footballers say. But in retrospect I'm glad that he said what he felt that he had to say and immensely grateful that he put his hand in his pocket to back his hunch that I really should have been a teacher. He was right. Professional football is a short career. There are heart-warming moments of glory, for sure, and ridiculous money is showered on those who make it in the top-flight today. Not in my day, however. You had to do something else to earn a living once you'd hung up your boots.

Thanks Shanks

Thanks to Shanks I've been able to do something that has been far more rewarding in the long-term – the very long-term as it has turned out. The D of E recently asked me to help to turn around a failing school in Birmingham. Every time I walk through the door there I feel a sense of anticipation, even excitement. And there aren't too many former professional footballers who can say that at 75.

Some Pictures from the Past

'Navy' David with his Mother

'Jack' Kershaw in his Navy Days

Family Holiday in Mablethorpe

David in the school Cricket Team

David in the school Football Team
in his goalkeeping days

Thanks Shanks

Vivien climbs aboard

Wedded bliss in Hereford

Pictures

Leaving Lancaster with pride

A more recent picture of Councillor Kershaw

Thanks Shanks

Lightning Source UK Ltd.
Milton Keynes UK
UKHW02f1259231117
313204UK00006B/190/P